Paul Johnson was born in 1928, educated at Stonyhurst and Magdalen College, Oxford, served as a captain in the British Army, edited the London *New Statesman* and has written over thirty books, of which the most recent is *A History of the American People*. His *Modern Times: A History of the World from the 1920s to the Year 2000* is a global bestseller which has been translated into a score of languages, and his *A History of Christianity* and *A History of the Jews* are standard works on five continents. Paul Johnson is a frequent contributor to newspapers throughout the world. He is married to the therapist Marigold Johnson, has four children and six grandchildren, and lives in London and Somerset.

By Paul Johnson

A History of the American People
Modern Times: A History of the World from the 1920s to the Year 2000
A History of Christianity
A History of the Jews
The Renaissance

Other titles in the Phoenix Press Universal History series

The Balkans *Mark Mazower*
Islam *Karen Armstrong*
Communism *Richard Pipes*
The German Empire 1871–1919 *Michael Stürmer*
The Catholic Church *Hans Küng*
Peoples and Empires *Anthony Pagden*
Hitler and the Holocaust *Robert Wistrich*

Contents

Chronology

Please note that some dates are approximate or speculative

1517 Luther begins Protestant Reformation

1525 Battle of Pavia

1533 Titian appointed court painter to the Emperor Charles V

1563 final session of Council of Trent

1564 death of Michelangelo

1588 death of Veronese

1594 death of Tintoretto

PART ONE

The Historical and Economic Background

The past is infinitely complicated, composed as it is of events, big and small, beyond computation. To make sense of it, the historian must select and simplify and shape. One way he shapes the past is to divide it into periods. Each period is made more memorable and easy to grasp if it can be labelled by a word that epitomizes its spirit. That is how such terms as 'the Renaissance' came into being. Needless to say, it is not those who actually live through the period who coin the term, but later, often much later, writers. The periodization and labelling of history is largely the work of the nineteenth century. The term 'Renaissance' was first prominently used by the French historian Jules Michelet in 1858, and it was set in bronze two years later by Jacob Burckhardt when he published his great book *The Civilisation of the Renaissance in Italy*. The usage stuck because it turned out to be a convenient way of describing the period of transition between the medieval epoch, when Europe was 'Christendom', and the beginning of the modern age. It also had some historical justification because, although the Italian elites of the time never used the words 'Renaissance' or 'Rinascita', they were conscious that a cultural rebirth of a kind was taking place, and that some of the literary, philosophical and artistic grandeur of ancient Greece and Rome was being recreated. In 1550 the painter Vasari published an ambitious work, *The Lives of the Artists*, in which he sought to describe how this process had taken place, and was continuing, in painting, sculpture and architecture. In comparing the glories of antiquity with the achievements of the present and recent past in Italy, he referred to the degenerate period in between as 'the middle ages'. This usage stuck too.

Thus a nineteenth-century term was used to mark the end of a period baptized in the sixteenth century. But when exactly, in real chronological terms, did this end of one epoch and beginning of another occur? Here we come to the first problem of the Renaissance. Historians have for long agreed that what they term the Early Modern Period of European history began at the end of the fifteenth century and the beginning of the sixteenth, though they date it differently in different countries. Thus, Spain entered the early modern age in 1492, when the conquest of Granada was completed with the expulsion of the Moors and the Jews, and Christopher Columbus landed in the western hemisphere on the instructions of Queen Isabella and King Ferdinand. England entered the period in 1485, when the last Plantagenet king, Richard III, was killed at Bosworth and the Tudor dynasty acquired the throne in the person of Henry VII. France and Italy joined Spain and England by virtue of the same event, in 1494, when the French king Charles VIII invaded Italy. Finally, Germany entered the new epoch in 1519, when Charles V united the imperial throne of Germany with the crown of Spain and the Indies. However, by the time these events took place, the Renaissance was already an accomplished fact, in its main outlines, and moving swiftly to what art historians term the High Renaissance, its culmination. Moreover, the next European epoch, the Reformation, usually dated by historians from Martin Luther's act in nailing his ninety-five theses to the door of the church in Wittenberg in 1517, had already begun. So we see that the connection between the Renaissance and the start of the early modern period is more schematic than chronologically exact.

The next problem, then, is defining the chronology of the Renaissance itself. If the term has any useful meaning at all, it signifies the rediscovery and utilization of ancient virtues, skills, knowledge and culture, which had been lost in the barbarous centuries following the collapse of the Roman Empire in the West, usually dated from the fifth century AD. But here we encounter another problem. Cultural rebirths, major and minor, are a common occurrence in history. Most generations, of all human societies, have a propensity to look back on golden ages and seek to restore them. Thus the long civilization of Ancient Egypt, neatly divided by modern archaeologists into the Old Kingdom, the Middle Kingdom and the New Kingdom, was punctuated by two collapses, termed intermediate periods, and both the Middle and the New Kingdoms were definite and systematic renaissances. Over three millennia, the cultural history of Ancient Egypt is marked by conscious archaisms, the deliberate revival of earlier patterns of art, architecture and literature to replace modes recognized as degenerate. This was a common pattern in ancient societies. When Alexander the Great created a world empire in the fourth century BC, his court artists sought to recapture the splendour of fifth-century Athenian civilization. So Hellenistic Greece, as we call it, witnessed a renaissance of classic values.

Rome itself periodically attempted to recover its virtuous and creative past. Augustus Caesar, while creating an empire on the eve of the Christian period, looked back to the noble spirit of the Republic, and even beyond it to the very origins of the City, to establish moral and cultural continuities, and so legitimize his regime. The court historian Livy resurrected the past in prose, the court epic poet Virgil told the story of Rome's divinely blessed origins in verse. The empire was never quite so self-confident as the Republic, subject as it was to the whims of a fallible autocrat, rather than the collective wisdom of the Senate, and it was always looking over its shoulder at a past that was more worthy of admiration, and seeking to resurrect its qualities. The idea of a Republican renaissance was never far from the minds of Rome's imperial elites.

Naturally, after the fall of the western empire in the fifth century AD, the longing for the recovery of the majestic past of Rome intensified among the fragile or semi-barbarous societies that succeeded the imperial order. In the Vatican Library there is a codex, known as the Roman Virgil, which dates from the fifth or sixth centuries. It is written in a monumental Capitalis Rustica, a self-conscious attempt to revive the Roman calligraphic majuscule, which had largely fallen out of use during the degenerate times of the third and fourth centuries. The artist-scribe, perhaps from Ravenna, who illustrated the text with miniatures, including one of Virgil himself, evidently had access to high-quality Roman work from a much earlier date, which he imitated and simplified to the best of his ability. Here is an early example of an attempted renaissance of lost Roman skills. There were many such.

A more successful and conscious renaissance, organized from

above, took place in and after the reign of Charlemagne, King of the Franks, 768–814, who brought together virtually all the Christian lands of Western Europe in one large kingdom. In the quasi-millennarian year AD 800 he had himself crowned emperor of what became established as the Holy Roman Empire, a Christian revival of the past distinguished from its pagan predecessor by its qualifying adjective. The coronation took place in Rome, during Christmas mass in Old St Peter's, Pope Leo III being the celebrant, but the new Roman emperor did not live there, preferring instead to erect a palace in his imperial heartland, Aachen. It was, however, built from materials transported from Rome and Ravenna, which had the right antique stamp and beauty. In Aachen Charlemagne created a court culture on what he believed to be Roman lines, having himself taught Latin and a little Greek, and summoning scholars to serve him from all over the known world. His chief intellectual assistant, Alcuin, wrote on Charlemagne's orders the *Epistola de Litteris colendis* (785), which outlined a programme for the study of the Latin language and texts sacred and profane at all the cathedral and monastic schools in the empire. A summary of the knowledge deemed authentic and needful, the *Libri Carolini*, was prepared and circulated. In Charlemagne's own scriptorium, and thereafter in other intellectual centres where his writ ran, his clerks developed what became known as the Carolingian minuscule, a clear and beautiful script, which became standard in the early Middle Ages.

There survive in the Vatican Library two codices that illustrate the impact of Charlemagne's programme. The first, the *Sacramentary Gelasianum*, dates from the period just before he came to the throne, and is distinguished by superb if barbarous paintings of plants and animals. It records ancient Roman liturgical ceremonies and other documentary evidence of the past, and is written in a fine uncial, though the minuscule that Charlemagne popularized makes its first appearance in places. This was the heritage on which the new emperor built. By contrast there is the far more sophisticated *Terentius Vaticanus*, dating from a few years after Charlemagne's death, written entirely in fine Carolingian minuscule and illustrated by paintings of actors performing Terence's plays. The book is interesting in itself as showing how familiar early medieval scholars were with Terence's writings, but the artwork is clearly and self-consciously based on earlier models from Roman times – the figures of actors in folio 55 recto, with their vigorous gestures, are powerful recapitulations of skills supposedly lost for centuries.

The Carolingian experiment had thus some of the characteristics of a genuine renaissance. But it remained an experiment. Ninth-century society lacked the administrative resources to sustain an empire the size of Charlemagne's, and anything less lacked the economic resources to consolidate and expand such an ambitious cultural programme. All the same, it was something to build on, and in due course the Ottonians of Germany, who also had themselves crowned Roman emperors in Rome, did so. By the eleventh century, the Holy Roman Empire, the successor-state (as it saw itself) to Rome, was a permanent element in medieval society, and a reminder that the achievements of Roman antiquity were not just a nostalgic memory but capable of re-creation. This was underlined visually by the spread of the architectural forms we call Romanesque, the sturdy round pillars, holding aloft semicircular arches, which early medieval masons, and their clerical employers, believed were characteristic of the architecture of imperial Rome at its best. Moreover, the Ottonian renaissance itself provoked a papal response, under the monk Hildebrand, enthroned as Pope Gregory VII. This included a fundamental refashioning of the entire corpus of canon law, on the lines of the great law-codes of late antiquity, and ambitious programmes for the education and moral improvement of the clergy, and their physical and intellectual liberation from the secular authorities. This naturally led to papal-imperial conflict, perpetuated in the political-military struggles of the Guelfs and the Ghibellines in Italy. But the positive side was that the Hildebrandine reforms spread under their own momentum into every part of western Christendom, producing a self-confident clerical class that included in its ranks a growing number of accomplished scholars.

In due course, the new scholars congregated in critical numbers to form what became known as universities, an extension and amalgamation of cathedral schools and monastic training centres.

The first emerged during the twelfth century in Paris, where Peter Lombard taught at the cathedral school of Notre-Dame, Abelard at St Geneviève and Hugh and Richard at St Victor. A similar development occurred in Oxford, where there is evidence from the second quarter of the twelfth century that independent masters were teaching Arts, Theology and Civil and Canon Law in schools grouped in the centre of the town. The new universities were the core of what we now call the Twelfth-Century Renaissance, and it is particularly significant that an arts faculty existed in Oxford as early as the 1120s because such courses provided the foundation for the true Renaissance more than 200 years later.

This proto-Renaissance was important not merely because it introduced qualitative improvements in the teaching, writing and spoken use of Latin, which became the lingua franca or hieratic tongue of a learned class composed mainly but not entirely of the clergy, but also because it was a quantitative explosion too. The growing number of scholars and literates stimulated a huge increase in the output of manuscripts from monastic scriptoria and secularized production centres in the towns. Some of the professional scribes were artists too, and their miniatures became a means by which artistic ideas circulated. Only the literate elites made use of codices and manuscripts but their illuminations were seen and used by church wall-painters, workers in stained glass, sculptors, masons and other artisans engaged in the enormous building and rebuilding programme which, beginning early in the twelfth century, transformed thousands of Romanesque churches and cathedrals into Gothic ones. It is worth noting that the new choir of Canterbury Cathedral, which replaced a Romanesque one after a fire in 1174, with a corona added to house the shrine of the murdered Thomas à Becket, included Corinthian columns, which we would date from fifteenth-century Italy, did we not possess documentary evidence that they were the work of William of Sens in the last quarter of the twelfth century.

With the new universities in place, the time and setting were ripe for the revival of Aristotle, the greatest encyclopaedist and systematic philosopher of antiquity. The early church fathers had regarded Aristotle with suspicion, ranking him as a materialist, in contrast to Plato, whom they saw as a more spiritual thinker and a genuine precursor of Christian ideas. Boethius in the sixth century expounded Aristotle with enthusiasm but he had few imitators, partly because the texts were known only in extracts or recensions. However, Aristotle's writings on logic began to circulate in the West from the ninth century, though they were not available in full until about 1130. The *Ethics* became available in Latin translation about 1200 and the *Politics* half a century later; and various scientific texts were translated from the Arabic, with learned Arabic commentaries, at the same time. Because of the transmission through Islam, Aristotle remained suspect in the church's eyes, as a possible source of heresy, but that did not stop the great thirteenth-century philosophers, Albertus Magnus and Thomas Aquinas, from constructing their *summae* on an Aristotelian basis. Indeed they, and particularly Aquinas, used Aristotle with brilliance, the net effect being to place Christian belief on a solid foundation of reason as well as faith. The incorporation of Aristotelian ideas and methods must be regarded as the first great complicated act in the long story of the recovery of the culture of antiquity, and it took place in the thirteenth century, before the Renaissance as such even began.

If so many elements of what constitutes the Renaissance were already in place even before the year 1300, why is it that the movement took so long to gather momentum and become self-sustaining? Here it is right to look for two explanations, one economic, one human. Athens in its prime was a rich trading centre, the centre of a network of maritime colonies; and the Alexandrine Empire that succeeded it was much larger and disposed of far greater resources; and the Roman Empire, which incorporated Alexander's as its eastern wing, was far larger still, and disposed of resources that have not been equalled until comparatively modern times. Such wealth made possible not only colossal public works programmes and generous state patronage of the arts but leisure classes of ample means who both patronized the arts and practised them. The Roman Empire was a monumental physical, legal and military fact, gathering and spending vast sums of money, from which the arts and literature incidentally benefited.

Once that monumental fact collapsed in irretrievable ruin,

caused in part by hyperinflation – the inability to maintain an honest currency – the gross economic product of the empire of the West's component parts declined steeply to a trough in the sixth and seventh centuries, from which it emerged only slowly, and with periodic regressions. Yet when the western economy did begin to gather strength, it did so on a basis that was fundamentally far more promising than anything that had existed in antiquity. The Greeks were inventive, and produced some scientists and engineers of genius, and the Romans were able to build on their work to carry out projects on a scale that is often impressive even by today's standards and appeared superhuman to medieval man. But there was something suspect about Roman monumentality. It was built on muscle-power rather than brain-power. The forts, the roads, the bridges, the enormous aqueducts, the splendid municipal and state buildings, were put up thanks to a conscript or servile multitude, whose human energies were the chief source of power. The slave gangs, constantly replenished by wars of conquest, were always available in almost unlimited numbers. The disincentive to develop new engineering skills, as opposed to the brute strength of immensely thick walls and buttresses, was continual. Indeed there is disconcerting evidence that the Roman authorities were reluctant to use labour-saving methods, even when available, for fear of unemployment and discontent. Considering the wealth of the Roman Republic in its prime, its technology was minimal, barely in advance of Athenian Greece, and confined largely to the military sphere. Yet even in the navy, the Romans made pitifully little use of sail-power, preferring oars rowed by galley slaves. Technology stagnated, and in the late empire, as inflation strengthened its grip, even regressed.

Medieval Europe had no such luxury in the use of manpower. Under the impact of Christian teaching, slavery declined slowly, then precipitously, especially in the Germanic north but later even in the Mediterranean south. By the time of the Domesday Book (1087) the number of slaves listed in England was tiny. Most men and women were *glebae adscripti*, tied to the soil of a particular place by elaborate feudal obligations, reinforced in time by statutory law, which forbade freedom of movement. It was difficult for villeins to flock to towns to constitute a labour market. Even unskilled labourers were in short supply, and ambitious building programmes soon ran into trouble on this account. When Edward I of England embarked on his huge castle-building effort in North Wales in the late thirteenth century, he found himself competing with the ecclesiastical authorities, who were rebuilding their cathedrals, for a limited pool of skilled draughtsmen and even for builders' labourers. The impact of labour scarcity is reflected in the rising costs recorded in the accounts of the King's Works. French experience was similar. The Black Death, in the mid-fourteenth century, by reducing the population of western Europe by twenty-five to thirty per cent, made labour still scarcer, even in agricultural areas, and seaports were hit too.

For all these reasons, there were strong incentives, which grew in the later Middle Ages, to improve labour-saving machinery and develop alternative sources of power to human muscles. Some of the medieval inventions were very simple, though important, like the wheelbarrow. The Romans had been extraordinarily slow in making effective use of the horse, making do with a type of ox-yoke or a harness consisting chiefly of a breast-band. In contrast, medieval farmers had developed, by the twelfth century, shafts, little used by the Romans, and traces; and they transformed the inefficient breast-band into the stiff, padded horse-collar, thereby multiplying the tractive power of the horse fivefold. To support the medieval knight, with his heavy armour, the French bred ever-stronger horses, which developed into the modern carthorse. These powerful animals, substituted for oxen at the plough, more than doubled agricultural productivity, and made it possible for farmers to substitute all-iron for wooden ploughs, thus raising it further. Such horses also pulled bigger carts, equipped with a swivelling front-axle, and more efficient concave wheels. In fourteenth-century England, cartage costs, where the return journey could be made in a day, fell to a penny per ton per mile, and more and more bridges made land travel, for the first time, competitive with water transport.

The Romans knew about the water-powered mill and they made some large specimens. But they were slow to build mills, preferring slaves, donkeys and horses to supply power; Vespasian, emperor 69–79 AD, was even said to have opposed the extension of water-power because it would throw men out of work. Shortage of iron also made the Romans reluctant to replace inefficient wooden gearing. In the Middle Ages, iron production increased steadily, making it cheaper and available for a variety of purposes, including gearing. Medieval forges also produced, for the first time, cast-iron, invaluable for harnessing power of all kinds. So thousands more watermills were built. In England, south of the Trent, the Domesday Book lists 5,624 watermills. Gradually, water-powered mills were used for sawing timber, fulling, ore-crushing, metal-hammering and mining. Their ubiquity and importance is reflected in complex laws governing the control of rivers. Moreover, from the twelfth century, water-power was joined by wind-power as a means of turning heavily geared metal-grinding machinery. Windmills, unknown to the Romans, were built in large numbers, and often of prodigious size. There were 8,000 in the Netherlands alone, where they were used not only for grinding corn but for pumping water, thus making possible drainage schemes that expanded the cultivable land area, a process taking place in many parts of Europe.

The complex sail-power used in the powering of windmills and the development of sail-power for ships were connected, and helped to explain why medieval mariners were able to improve so markedly on Roman sea transport, largely confined to the oar-propelled galley. The cog, driven entirely by sail, made its appearance in the thirteenth century, chiefly in the northern waters of the Hanseatic League. It was succeeded in the fourteenth century by the Portuguese caravels, lateen-rigged ships with two or three masts, multiple decks and a big hull – in all essentials modern sailing ships – often weighing 600 tons or more and carrying their own weight in cargo. This vessel was capable of sailing into and across Atlantic seas, and eventually did so, aided by the invention of the magnetic compass, mechanical timepieces and navigational charts, which were improving all the time.

With revolutionized sea-power and improved land transport, internal and external trade in Europe virtually doubled with each generation. Overseas trade, especially with the East, made plague more common, and outbreaks, such as the Black Death (1348–9), decimated the population. But there is no evidence that plague interrupted the wealth-producing process. It more likely accelerated it in the long run by providing yet more incentives to the use of non-human power, metals and labour-saving devices. At the same time the expansion of trade produced ancillary practices, such as insurance and banking, on an ever-growing scale, aided by the invention of techniques such as double-entry book-keeping.

Thus in the later Middle Ages, wealth was being produced in greater quantities than ever before in history, and was often concentrated in cities specializing in the new occupations of large-scale commerce and banking, like Venice and Florence. Such cities were chiefly to be found in the Low Countries, the Rhine valley and in northern and central Italy. As wealth accumulated, those who possessed it gratified their senses by patronizing literature and the arts, and they were joined by sovereigns, popes and princes, who found ways of taxing the new wealth of their subjects. But wealth alone would not have produced the phenomenon we call the Renaissance. Money can command art, but it commands in vain if there are no craftsmen to produce it. Happily, there is evidence everywhere that Europe, in the later Middle Ages, was entering a period of what modern economists call intermediate technology. Especially in the Low Countries, Germany and Italy, thousands of workshops of all kinds emerged, specializing in stone, leather, metal, wood, plaster, chemicals and fabrics, producing a growing variety of luxury goods and machinery. It was chiefly the families of those who worked in these shops who produced the painters and carvers, the sculptors and architects, the writers and decorators, the teachers and scholars responsible for the huge expansion of culture that marked the beginnings of the early modern age.

There was one respect in which the growth of intermediate technology had a direct, indeed explosive, effect on this cultural spread. Indeed, it was the most important cultural event by far of the entire period. This was the invention, followed by the extraordinarily rapid diffusion, of printing. The Romans produced a large literature. But in publishing it they were, as in many other fields, markedly conservative. They knew about the codex – that is, a collection of folded and cut sheets, sewn together and enclosed within a binding – but they clung onto the old-fashioned scroll as the normative form of book. It was the early Christians who preferred the codex, and the replacement of the scroll by ever more sophisticated codices was the work of the so-called Dark Ages. What the Christians took from the Romans was a version of their screw winepress, to bind the codex.

The material on which the Romans originally wrote was papyrus, the dried leaves of a grass grown along the Nile, and it is from this term that our word paper is ultimately derived. But between 200 BC and 300 AD papyrus was replaced by vellum, calfskin soaked in lime, then smoothed by knife and pumice stone, or parchment, made from the scraped skin of sheep or goats. Vellum was a luxury material, extremely durable, and was used throughout the Middle Ages for the finest manuscripts. Indeed, it continued to be used in the Renaissance, even for printed work, though special care was required to produce satisfactory results. Parchment was cheaper but also durable and continued to be used for certain legal documents until the mid-twentieth century. However, during the Middle Ages both were largely superseded by paper, or cloth-parchment as it was originally called. This was an industrial process to turn fibrous material, such as straw, wood, linen or cotton, into pulp, which was then spread in sheets over a wire framework. It came from China via the Moslem world, from which it reached Spain and Sicily. By about 1150 the Spanish had improved on the original process by developing a stamp mill, turned by hand, which used a wheel and tappets to raise and drop pestles in mortars. By the thirteenth century, paper mills were powered by water, and leadership in the industry had shifted to Italy, which by 1285 had developed the practice of sewing a figure of wire into the mould to produce a watermark. Efficiently produced, paper was cheaper than any other writing material by far. Even in England, which was backward in the trade, a sheet of paper (eight octavo pages) cost only one penny by the fifteenth century.

The availability of cheap paper in growing quantities was a key factor in making the invention of printing by movable type the central technological event in the Renaissance. Printing from wooden blocks was an old idea: the Romans used the technique for textiles and the Mongol Empire used it to make paper currency. By about 1400, playing cards and pictures of saints were being printed from blocks in Venice and southern Germany. The key novelty, however, was the invention of movable type for letter-press, which had three advantages: it could be used repeatedly until worn out; it could be easily renewed, being cast from a mould; and it introduced strict uniformity of lettering. Movable type was the work of two Mainz goldsmiths, Johann Gutenberg and Johann Fust, in the years 1446–8. In 1450 Gutenberg began work on a printed Bible, known as the Gutenberg Bible or the Forty-two Line Bible (from the number of lines on the pages), which was completed in 1455 and is the world's first printed book. Gutenberg had to solve all the problems of punch cutting, type foundings, composing the type, imposing the paper and ink, and the actual printing, for which he used a modification of the screw-press. The resulting book, which amazes those who first see and handle it for its clarity and quality, is a triumph of fifteenth-century German craftsmanship at its best.

Printing from movable type, therefore, was a German invention, which rather undermines the label 'the Italian Renaissance'. Germans were quick to exploit the new possibilities, for religious books, especially Bibles, and works of reference, but also for scarce classic texts. The first printed encyclopaedia, the *Catholicon*, appeared in 1460 and the following year a Strasbourg printer, Johann Mentelin, produced a Bible for laymen. He followed this with a Bible in German, the first printed book in the vernacular. Cologne had its own press by 1464, Basle two years later. Basle quickly became famous for scholarly editions of the classics, later with Desiderius Erasmus, the Dutch humanist, as their literary adviser. Nuremburg got its first press in 1470 and soon became the earliest centre of the international printing trade, where Anton Koberger worked twenty-four presses and had a network of con-nections with traders and scholars all over Europe. In Augsburg the new presses were built alongside the Abbey of St Ulrich, which had one of the most famous scriptoria in Europe. There seems to have been little commercial conflict between the scriptoria and the new presses, the scriptoria concentrating on luxury books of ever-increasing complexity and beauty, often illustrated by leading artists, the printers on quantity and cheapness. Thus the first best-seller in the new world of print was Thomas à Kempis's *De imitatione Christi*, which went through ninety-nine editions in the thirty years from 1471 to 1500.

Though the Italians were not the first into printing, with their large paper-making industry, their experience in block printing and their strong scriptoria tradition, they soon took the leadership in the new technology. Near Rome, the Benedictine monastery of Subiaco had links with Germany, and in 1464–5 it commissioned two German printers, Sweynheym and Pannartz, to set up presses alongside its scriptorium. Presses in Germany had one important disadvantage in international trade. Gutenberg and other German printers based their type on imitations of the calligraphic strokes of official writing, using German Gothic hands of the mid-fifteenth century as their model (known later in England as 'Black Letter' type). Outside Germany, readers found these typefaces repellent and difficult to understand. The German printers of the Subiaco press were ordered to cut type based on the standard style of handwriting used by Italian humanists in the fifteenth century, itself based on the admirably clear Carolingian minuscule. This became known as Roman, and was the true Renaissance type.

Nicholas Jenson, the Master of the Royal Mint at Tours, was sent by King Charles VII of France to Mainz in 1468 to learn the new art of printing. But instead of returning to France, Jenson spent the rest of his life in Venice, where he set up the most famous printing press in the world. He cut superb examples of Roman types, which were imitated all over Europe. From 1490 his presses were rivalled in Venice by those of Aldus Manutius, who not only designed a serviceable Greek type, for printing ancient texts in the original, but who also designed and popularized a type based on the cursive handwriting used in the fifteenth-century papal chancery. This is characterized by a sharp inclination to the right and exaggerated serifs, and the type based on it became known as Italic. Aldus used it first in 1501, upper-case only. Lower-case followed around 1520 and some books were produced entirely in Italic. Later it slipped comfortably into its modern role of use for emphasis, contrast and quotation.

The speed at which printing spread, the quality and quantity of the production, and the extraordinary mechanical ingenuity displayed, together constituted a kind of industrial revolution. By 1500, less than half a century after the first printed book, there were printing firms in sixty German towns, and Venice alone had 150 presses. German workmen took printing to Utrecht in the Netherlands in 1470, Budapest in Hungary in 1473 and Cracow in Poland in 1474. Printing reached Valencia in Spain in 1473, and a quarter-century later, under the patronage of Cardinal Francisco Jimenez de Cisneros, Spain began to produce what remains to this day one of the most remarkable books ever devised, the Complutensian Polyglot Bible, in five languages of antiquity, Hebrew, Syriac, Latin, Greek and Chaldee, the texts running in parallel columns. At the other end of the market, Manutius was producing cheap Latin texts for the use of poor scholars. The spread of printing in the vernacular was one way in which the market expanded. Thus William Caxton, who learned printing in Cologne and ran his first press at Bruges in 1474, brought printing to England in 1476 with an eye to the vernacular readership. Of the ninety or so books he published, seventy-four were in English, of which twenty-two were his own translations.

The printed book trade, then, might be described as the first really efficient and innovative pan-European industry. Advertisements for books began to appear in 1466, and publishers' catalogues soon afterwards. The quantitative impact was overwhelming. Before printing, only the very largest libraries contained as many as 600 books, and the total number in Europe was well under 100,000. By 1500, after forty-five years of the printed book, the total has been calculated at nine million.

Hence, the background to what we call the Renaissance was a cumulative growth and spread of wealth never before experienced in world history, and the rise of a society in which intermediate technology was becoming the norm, producing in due course a startling revolution in the way words were published and distributed. But this does not mean the Renaissance was an economic, let alone a technological, event. Without economic and technological developments it could not have taken the form it did, and so it has been necessary to describe the material background first. But it must be grasped that the Renaissance was primarily a human event, propelled forward by a number of individuals of outstanding talent, which in some cases amount to genius. We turn now to the human foreground, and in the first place to the writers.

PART TWO

The Renaissance in Literature and Scholarship

The Renaissance was the work of individuals, and in a sense it was about individualism. And the first and greatest of those individuals was Dante Alighieri (1265–1321). Dante was a Florentine, appropriately because Florence played a more important role in the Renaissance than any other city. He also embodies the central paradox of the Renaissance: while it was about the recovery and understanding of ancient Greek and Latin texts, and the writing of elegant Latin, it was also about the maturing, ordering and use of vernacular languages, especially Italian. We know little about Dante's early life, except that his parents died before he was eighteen. He was betrothed at twelve and married in 1293, when he was twenty-eight. In typical Italian fashion, this was a family matter of little emotional significance. His emotional life began in 1274, aged nine, it is believed, when he first glimpsed his Beatrice (Bice Portinari, the daughter of a respectable Florentine citizen). His poetical life was devoted to her presence and after 1290, when she died, to her memory; in a sense, his entire life and work was dedicated to her.

There were three key elements in Dante's education. One was the Florentine Dominicans with whom he studied in the 1290s. By then the great Dominican teacher and writer, St Thomas Aquinas, was dead, his work complete, so Dante was able to absorb the whole Aristotelian philosophy, as received and Christianized by Aquinas. Thomist Aristotelianism gives a structure to his oeuvre, bringing to it internal consistency and intellectual rigour. Second, Dante had as mentor the classical scholar Brunetto Latini. He too was an Aristotelian, and the first part of Book Two of his main work, *Li Livres dou Trésor*, written in French because Italian was not yet regarded as a suitable tongue for a serious work, contains a translation of Aristotle's *Ethics*, one of the first in a European vernacular. It was thanks to Brunetto Latini that

Dante was able to understand the importance of rhetoric, that is, the ability to present a case and to use Latin – or any other language – with force and elegance. Through Latini, too, Dante got to know at least part of the work of Cicero and Seneca. Virgil, and especially his *Aeneid*, the epic successor to Homer's *Iliad* and *Odyssey*, had never gone out of use even in the more harassed period of the Dark Ages, and had always found Christian defenders. But other Christians, including some of the weightiest, like St Jerome and St Augustine, had condemned him as a pagan archetype. Latini, however, taught Dante that Virgil was to be used as well as enjoyed, and in Dante's *Divine Comedy*, which can be seen as a Christian successor to the *Aeneid*, Virgil appears as his guide through Hell and Purgatory, though Dante is sufficiently orthodox a Christian to exclude him from Paradise, allowing the Latin poet to sink into Limbo instead.

The third element in Dante's education was the influence and encouragement of his friend and near-contemporary Cavalcanti, another classical scholar but a man whose passion was the promotion of Italian. It was he who persuaded Dante to write in the Tuscan or Florentine version of the Italian tongue. In due course, Dante provided in his *Convivio*, written in Italian, and in his *De vulgari eloquentia*, written in Latin, the first great Renaissance defence of the vernacular as a suitable language for works of beauty and weight. The *De vulgari* contains a sentence which prophesies of Italian: 'This shall be the new light, the new sun, which rises when the worn-out one shall set, and shall give light to them who are in shadow and darkness because of the old sun, which did not enlighten them' – a shrewd recognition, on his part, that the masses would never acquire a significant grasp of Latin but could be taught to read their own spoken tongue. More important than his arguments, however, was the example he provided, in the *Divine Comedy*, written throughout in Italian, that the common Tuscan tongue could be used to write the most exquisite poetry and to deal with matter of the highest significance. Before Dante, Tuscan was one of many Italian dialects and there was no Italianate written language that was accepted throughout the peninsula. After Dante, however, written Italian (in the Tuscan mode) was a fact. Indeed, Italians of the twenty-first century, and foreigners who have some grasp of Italian, can read most of the *Divine Comedy* without difficulty. No other writer has ever had such a decisive impact on a modern language.

Dante's *Divine Comedy*, describing his journey through Hell, Purgatory and Heaven, and what he saw therein, is a Christian epic about vice and virtue, rewards and punishments. It has an enormous cast of characters, many of them Dante's contemporaries. In 1294 he became involved in politics in Florence, a city that was itself highly political, deeply committed to the Guelf or papal cause. Florence itself was split into two parties, as were most Italian cities, and the party to which Dante belonged, having opposed the ultra-triumphalist Pope Boniface VIII, lost the game, and he was exiled in 1301, a sentence renewed in 1315. These Italian city faction-fights were vicious and deadly. Dante had his property confiscated and was condemned to be burned at the stake if he returned to the city. He spent much of his life, therefore, in exile, chiefly in Ravenna, where he died, and he laments in pitiful verse the pain of 'eating another man's bread and using another man's stair to go to bed'.

Yet there is little bitterness in his great *Commedia*. Dante was a man of exceptional magnanimity, of all-encompassing love for mankind as well as individuals; and he understood, too, the nature of divine love, which suffuses the universe and gives it meaning. His poem is moralistic and didactic, as plainly so in many ways as a great altarpiece in a medieval cathedral. He takes the Christian faith with awesome seriousness and does not seek to discount the miseries of the damned or the pains of purgatory. In this sense he was a medieval man, built to be sure on a gigantic scale, but untouched by doubt about the mechanics of the universe as described by the church. But he was also a storyteller of immense resources, and a poet of genius. The narrative moves forward at a great pace and is full of delightful, striking and terrifying incidents, lit by flashes of vivid verbal colour and what can only be called inspiration.

Moreover, Dante was not just medieval man; he was Renaissance man too. He was highly critical of the church, like so many scholars who followed him. Although a Guelf, he was impressed by the German Emperor Henry VII, who came to Italy in 1310 and converted Dante to the idea of a universal monarchy, expressed in a Latin treatise *De Monarchia*, condemned as heretical after the poet's death. Dante had great faith. He grasped the point of medieval Christendom, that the only way to personal peace was submission to the divine will, however hard it was at times to bear. But he had the critical spirit of the new times that were coming. He saw into the heart of things with a piercing gaze. All men (and women), rich and poor, well or badly educated, could find something in him, and read or listened to his verse with wonder. His fame came soon after his death, and continued to grow steadily. Soon, Florence, which had expelled him, was fighting with Ravenna for custody of his honourable, and now highly valuable, bones. Dante not only launched the Italian language as a vehicle for high art; in a sense he launched the Renaissance itself, as a new era of creative endeavour by individuals of unprecedented gifts. He became a model, a beacon, a mentor, as Virgil was to him, an energizing, vivifying source for talents of a lesser order and a towering giant against whom the most ambitious could measure themselves. After Dante, nothing seemed beyond human reach.

That was the view of another Tuscan, Giovanni Boccaccio, born in 1313 when Dante still had some time to live, and destined by his merchant-father for a life of business. For this purpose he was sent to Naples, but there he found, like Dante, his lifelong love, Fiammetta, who emerges in all his work, like a palimpsest. He was Dante's heir, in his ability to handle the newly mature language, and in his surpassing ability to tell a tale. His mother was French, and he subsumed in his work the legacy of the French medieval romances. He took the *ottava rima* of the minstrels and gave it literary status, made it indeed the most dynamic verse-form in Italian literature. His *Decameron*, second only to the *Divine Comedy* as a source of delight for Renaissance Europe, is a product of the Black Death of 1348. The author has seven young women and three young men flee from Florence to escape infection. They remain in the countryside a fortnight, ten days of which are spent storytelling, making a hundred tales in all. Each story ends with a *canzone* or song. It is thus a compendium of stories and verse, which less inventive spirits ransacked for inspiration over the next two centuries. The church and the stiffer element in society did not like it, for it represents the more liberal approach to lifestyles and opinion of the younger generation, contrasted with the formalities and stuffiness of the past. The rest liked it for precisely this reason. It is thus a 'progressive' book, the harbinger of a growing Renaissance trend.

Boccaccio exhibits a characteristic Renaissance ability to do a great many different things, all with skill and panache. He served as a municipal councillor, and as an ambassador on numerous occasions, to the pope and in Germany; he was a man of the world and courtier, but also a scholar as well as a writer. His energy was prodigious and his output vast. For nearly forty years a team of Italian scholars have been producing a massive collective edition of it, with a full critical apparatus, revealing perhaps for the first time the scale and range of his work. His first novel, *Filocolo*, once dismissed as a minor work, is actually over 600 printed pages and was read all over Europe. He wrote nine other considerable works of fiction in Italian. He produced in homage a life of Dante, which circulated widely in various editions and abridgements. But he drove himself far more deeply than the master into the emerging corpus of antique literature. Between 1360 and 1362, he gave lodgings to Leonzio Pilato, and got him made Reader in Greek at the Studio, the old name for the University of Florence. He saw to it that Pilato made a rough translation into Latin of Homer, the means whereby he and many others (including Petrarch) began their journey into the Greek literary classics. He helped the process of recovering authentic texts of Martial, Apulius, Varro, Seneca, Ovid and Tacitus. Indeed, the rediscovery of Tacitus was mainly his doing. He translated Livy into Italian. He produced a number of reference works, including two massive classical encyclopaedias. One is a topography of the ancient world, listing all the places such as woods, springs, lakes and seas mentioned in Greek and Latin literature, arranged alphabetically. To do this he used the elder Pliny, various Roman geographers like Pomponius Mela and Vibius Sequester, and the classical texts, descanting rapturously for example on Virgil's birthplace at Petola.

More important still was his great compilation, *The Geneal-*

ogies of the Pagan Gods, which sorted out all the confusing deities referred to in the classics of antiquity. Sometimes he misread or misunderstood texts, thus producing pure inventions, like Demogorgon, who went on to pursue a vigorous life of his own. But most people eager to understand the literature of the past found these volumes godsends. They became mines of information and inspiration not just for scholars and writers but, perhaps even more so, for artists, looking for subjects. By writing at such length about the pagan deities, Boccaccio risked falling foul of the church, and defended himself by saying that the men and women whom the pagans worshipped were not gods at all but merely exceptional humans whose exploits had been immortalized by endless recounting. They thus posed no threat to Christian theology. In fact, like so much else of the material supplied by the Renaissance recovery of antiquity, Boccaccio's work constituted a real challenge to the Christian monopoly of the incidents that artists portrayed. Up to the second half of the fourteenth century, their subject-matter was almost entirely Christian. They continued, of course, to use episodes in the life of Christ and the saints, and scenes from the Old Testament until the end of the seventeenth century and beyond. But they now had an alternative, and in some ways a more attractive one, because classical mythology provided many more opportunities for the display of beauty – particularly female flesh – and of *joie de vivre* than the endless Christian stress on piety and the sufferings of the martyrs. This was one way in which the church's iron grip on visual art, and so on the minds of simple men and women who could not read, was gradually prised loose.

That was not Boccaccio's intention, far from it. His frivolous youth, during which his best fiction was produced, was succeeded by an increasingly thoughtful and even pious maturity and old age. It is a fact we have to recognize that these masters of the fourteenth and fifteenth centuries, and even later, waxed and waned in the intensity of their religious passions. Behind an increasingly this-worldly Renaissance veneer, there was a medieval substructure, which emerged powerfully when the veneer wore thin, as it tended to do with age. From Dante onwards, these great men had one foot in the exciting Renaissance present, and the other firmly placed in the medieval past, with its superstitions and credal certitudes.

The split personality, the Janus-face, the rival tugging of past, present and future were epitomized in Boccaccio's lifelong comrade, Francesco Petrarch (1304–74). He was older than his friend, better educated, pursued an intermittent career in the service of the papacy, then in exile in Avignon, and was a far more dedicated and gifted poet. He too had a muse, Laura (and also, while holding a canonry, sired a daughter). But whilst Dante was essentially an epic poet, Petrarch was a lyricist. His fourteen-line sonnet still survives as a form, and he invented others. He could compose and arrange short lyrics in sequence and gather them together in a coherent anthology. Thus he aspired to revive the cult of poetry, as the highest art form, after what he saw as a gap of an entire millennium. The world recognized his efforts and in 1341 he was publicly crowned poet on the Capitoline Hill in Rome, like his antique predecessors, though he was careful to deposit the laurel wreath on the tomb of St Peter in the ancient basilica bearing his name.

Petrarch was directly concerned with the rebirth of classical culture by hunting down manuscripts of lost classics in old monastic libraries. It is often said that the Renaissance was fuelled by the arrival of manuscripts from Byzantium. So it was. But most of classic literature had been there all the time, in crumbling scrolls and ancient codices covered with dust, preserved – if barely – by pious but ignorant monks who knew not what treasures they guarded. Petrarch was much more widely travelled than either Dante or Boccaccio. In 1333 he voyaged through the Rhineland, Flanders, Brabant and France, meeting scholars and ransacking libraries. In Liège, for instance, he discovered copies of two lost speeches by Cicero. At Verona in 1345 he stumbled on a far more dramatic find, Cicero's letters to Atticus, Brutus and Quintus – texts that brought the great orator to life for the first time. This discovery persuaded Petrarch to take more trouble with his own letters, and he thus became responsible for the revival of another art form. His own letters were preserved, collected and edited, then in due course published. Petrarch liked scholarly seclusion as well as furious activity and gregariousness.

He had a country retreat in the Vaucluse, and later at Aequa in the hills near Venice, where his delightful house, beloved of Byron, Shelley and other Romantic poets, conjures up his spirit to the modern visitors who trouble to go there – it is the Renaissance itself, in brick and plaster and stone, though not without a whispering of the Middle Ages too.

Even more evocative, however, and more suggestive of what the early Renaissance was all about, are the manuscripts that survive in Petrarch's own hand. He was not only a great poet but a calligrapher – an artist indeed – of professional skill. Three manuscripts in particular, all in the Vatican Library, testify to his passion for the act of writing. In 1357, he transcribed his 'Bucolicum Carmen' in a superb Gothic minuscule. The writing is in black, with some capitals in blue, and a sentence at the end, in red, testifies that the hand is his. In 1370 he used an even finer Gothic book minuscule to transcribe the whole of his codex, *De sui imsius et multorum ignorantia*, noting his work ('scripsi his iterum manu mea') on the verso of its thirty-eighth folio. Even more spectacular is the original manuscript of his collection of verses, the *Canzoniere* or song-book. This is also in a Gothic book minuscule, but not all of the writing is Petrarch's, a professional scriptor being responsible for some of it. On the other hand, the recto of the first folio has a first initial decorated with multi-coloured branches and leaves, in Petrarch's hand, and he continued to correct and embellish the manuscript until his death. The whole of the early Renaissance lives on in this noble page from the poet's mind and nimble fingers.

Petrarch may be called the first humanist, and he was certainly the first author to put into words the notion that the centuries between the fall of Rome and the present had been an age of darkness. In the medieval university, the seven 'humanities' had been the least-regarded subjects of study. Petrarch placed them first, and he laid them out as follows. First came grammar, based upon study of the languages of antiquity as the ancients had used them (including the correct pronunciation). This involved the careful study and imitation of the great classical authors. Once the language was mastered grammatically, you could use it to attain the second stage, eloquence or rhetoric. This art of persuasion was not art for its own sake, but the acquisition of the capacity to persuade others – all men and women – to lead the good life. As Petrarch put it, 'It is better to will the good than to know the truth.' Rhetoric thus led to, and embraced, philosophy. Leonardo Bruni (1369–1444), the outstanding scholar of the new generation, insisted that it was Petrarch who 'opened the way for us to show how to acquire learning', but it was in Bruni's time that the word *umanista* first came into use, and its subjects of study were listed as five: grammar, rhetoric, poetry, moral philosophy and history.

It is important to grasp that at no time before the Reformation did the humanists acquire a dominant position at the established universities, which continued to be organized around the study of theology, 'the queen of the sciences', and whose teaching methods were shaped accordingly. The humanists disliked, and reacted against, not only the curriculum of the universities but their reliance on the highly formalized academic technique of public debate and questions and answers to impart knowledge. They rightly saw it as inefficient, time-wasting and so entailing long courses, of seven years or more (a theology student could not normally hope to get his doctorate until at least thirty-five, at a time when the average lifespan was forty years or less). The method also made it difficult for master and pupil to establish a close relationship – and the notion of friendship in study was at the heart of the humanist love of letters.

Hence the humanists were outsiders, and to some extent non-academics. They associated universities with the kind of closed-shop trades unionism also found in the craft guilds. Universities, in their view, stamped on individualism and innovation. Humanist scholars tended to wander from one centre of learning to another, picking their choice fruits, then moving on. They set up their own little academies. In 1423, Vittorino da Feltre founded a school in Mantua that taught the new humanist curriculum. Six years later Guarino da Verona did the same in Ferrara. Humanists penetrated universities as a kind of subversive, protesting element. But they also attached themselves to noble and princely households, which could make their own rules and were often avid to embrace cultural novelty. One of the ablest of the humanists,

THE RENAISSANCE

Angelo Poliziano (1454–94), who wrote under the professional humanist name of Politian, became tutor to the Medici children, though he was also professor at the Florence Studio.

Politian belonged to a mid-fifteenth-century generation that took it for granted that a humanist scholar had some knowledge of Greek. Dante and Boccaccio knew no Greek. Petrarch knew a little, just enough to fill him with anguish that he did not know more, and to allow him to perceive that, in Greek literature of antiquity, there was a treasure-house surpassing anything in Latin. In the later Middle Ages, Greek was quite unlike Latin in one important respect: it was still a living language, albeit in debased form, in the Byzantine Empire. That too, was debased and shrunken. The Italians, or Latins as the Byzantines called them, saw Constantinople, the capital, as a repository of marvels from antiquity, rather than a living cultural centre. Contemporary Byzantine art was a static, moribund tradition, from which Italian artists in the Middle Ages had to struggle to free themselves. The Venetians exploited the Fourth Crusade at the beginning of the thirteenth century to occupy Constantinople, which they saw as a trading rival, and pillage it, stealing the four great bronze antique horses they found there, and placing them triumphantly over the arcade of their cathedral, St Mark's.

Constantinople was also known in the West to contain depositories of ancient Greek literature, and a few scholars familiar with it. In 1397 the Greek scholar Manuel Chrysoloras was invited to lecture in Florence, and it was from this point that classical Greek began to be studied seriously, and widely, in the West. One Italian scholar, Garino da Verona, actually went to Constantinople, and spent some years there, in the circle of Chrysoloras. He returned to Italy in 1408, not only fluent in Greek but with an important library of fifty-four Greek manuscripts, including some of the works of Plato, hitherto unknown in the West. The rest of Plato was brought from Constantinople in the 1420s by Giovanni Aurispa. This was the first great transmission of classical Greek literature. The second occurred during the ecumenical council of Florence in the 1430s, an attempt to heal the schism between the Latin and Greek Churches. The attempt failed, but the Greek delegation, which included a number of distinguished scholars, brought with them many important manuscripts that remained in Florence. A third batch arrived in the baggage of refugees, escaping from Turkish rule to the West in the wake of the fall of Constantinople in 1453. Meanwhile, the rediscovery of Latin classics continued with the work of, among others, Poggio Bracciolini (1380–1459), an indefatigable ransacker of monastic libraries in Europe, who brought to light more Cicero, Quintilian and other authors.

One reason why the humanists, while failing to dominate the old universities, got such a grip on society, was their ability to infiltrate courts. They ran, in effect, a scholastic freemasonry, getting each other jobs and recommendations, and chances to acquire patronage from the rich and powerful. Bracciolini, like Petrarch, worked in the papal service and attended the Council of Constance, 1414–18, where much trafficking in manuscripts was done. He also worked for a time for the English grandee, Cardinal Beaufort. The humanists had ready pens, which could be used for political purposes, either in Latin or in the vernacular. Coluccio Salutati (1351–1402) was made Chancellor of Florence, whose interest he defended fiercely with his literary skills. The Visconti of Milan claimed that his pen had done more damage than 'thirty squadrons of Florentine cavalry', to which the Chancellor replied, 'I would not restrain my words on occasions when I would not fail to use my sword.' Humanists were prominent in Florentine government, being chosen as chancellor on four occasions. Leonardo Bruni, for instance, who acquired administrative and diplomatic experience at the papal curia, and was also the author of a laudatory history of Florence, based on classical models, was elected chancellor in 1427. When he died in 1444 the city ignored his will, which asked for a modest funeral and a simple slab gravestone, and gave him state obsequies on the Roman model, and commissioned an elaborate Renaissance monument, on classical lines, from the sculptor Bernardo Rossellino, over his vault in the Franciscan church of Santa Croce.

Behind this interest of the great and powerful in humanist scholarship was not just the itch to acquire propagandists but the desire to recreate the externals of imperial Rome – the Latin slogans, the sumptuary, the designs and insignia – in the expectation that the reality of Roman power would follow. The imitation of antiquity became the fashion. The private academy founded in Rome by Pomponio Leto (1428–98) not only studied ancient history but on occasions wore Roman dress, held Roman feasts, collected inscriptions and staged discussions *alla romana*, even tending their gardens according to classical principles gathered from Virgil and Horace. In Florence, the Medici went further, erecting the recovery of classical antiquity almost into a principle of government. Indeed, it is important to grasp that their power in Florence in the fifteenth century, though ultimately based on their money – they were a family of doctors turned bankers – was expressed by cultural leadership, for they had no formal authority or legal title until 1537, when Cosimo de' Medici I (1519–74) became Duke of Florence and ultimately Grand Duke of Tuscany. It was through their cultural enthusiasm for the new, the perfect and the magnificent, that they identified themselves with the fortunes of the city, which by about the year 1400 had become, self-consciously and emotionally, a citadel of the arts.

The pattern was set by Cosimo de' Medici (1389–1464), who dominated Florentine public life for an entire generation. Of course he was rich: his father's personal wealth, over 80,000 florins in 1427, could have paid – it was estimated – the annual wages of 2,000 workers in the wool industry. But he was also an enthusiastic would-be scholar. In 1427 he was in Rome helping Poggio Bracciolini to find antique inscriptions. He commissioned and paid for the translation of Plato by Marsilio Ficino, which was presented in one of the finest manuscripts of the whole Renaissance. At one point he was employing no less than thirty-five professional scriptors in copying classics for his library. It was, significantly, his bookseller, Vespasiano da Bisticci, who wrote his *Life*, in which he asserted: 'He had a knowledge of Latin which was astonishing in a man engrossed by public affairs.' He also used his money to complete the church of San Lorenzo, the Badia church outside Fiesole, the library and monastery of San Marco and add to the Franciscan church of Santa Croce – all public projects – as well as building the family palace in Florence, designed by Michelozzo, and patronizing all the leading masters, from Donatello down. This was in addition to subsidizing Florence's armies and diplomacy to the point where, at the Peace of Lodi in 1454, the city was recognized as one of Italy's five major powers, alongside Venice, the papacy, Milan and Naples.

Cosimo's grandson, Lorenzo 'the Magnificent' (1449–92), while ruling Florence in fact though not in name, and with a rod not so much of iron as of gold and ivory, went one better than Cosimo. He was not only a scholar, and patron of scholars, supporting the work of Ficino, like his grandfather, and of Pico della Mirandola and Angelo Poliziano in the translation and editing of Latin and Greek texts, but he was also a poet of distinction. His model was Petrarch, but his verses are full of original ideas, conceits and forms. They celebrate hunting, the woods, nature, the love of women; they deplore the brevity and transience of life; they exude joy and bawdy as well as sadness. They were read widely when first published; some are still read and enjoyed today. Lorenzo commissioned works from most of the great painters and sculptors of his day – Verrocchio, Ghirlandaio, the Pollaiuoli and Botticelli – and he built on a monumental scale. His son Giovanni became Pope Leo X and his nephew, Giulio, Clement VII. His great-granddaughter Catherine married one king of France and was mother of three more. Yet Lorenzo was, as some would claim, the key figure in the entire Renaissance, and the nearest to approach its ideal of the *uomo universale*, chiefly because he was also an author in his own right.

The Medici of Florence were not the only ruling family who identified themselves with the new culture – fortunately so, for it was the very competitiveness of the independent cities, and the regimes and rulers who strove to bolster their power with the embellishments of scholarship and art, that gave the Renaissance its thrust. It was one of the few times in human history when success in the world's game – the struggle for military supremacy and political dominion – was judged at least in part on cultural performance. Often cultural patronage (like hypocrisy) was the homage that vice paid to virtue. Italian city rulers were often ruthless. Bernabò Visconti, who consolidated the power of his family in Milan in the fourteenth century, was barbarously cruel, and his nephew Giangaleazzo (1351–1402) was an unscrupulous operator who extended Milan's rule to cover the whole of Lombardy, parts of Piedmont and even slices of Tuscany. But he was a generous and discerning collector, a friend of scholars and a patron of the new learning. The Sforza family, who succeeded the Visconti in Milan, were notable patrons of Leonardo da Vinci and Bramante. Another humanist city was Ferrara, controlled by the d'Este family.

It was a characteristic of humanism to pay almost as much attention to the education of ladies as of gentlemen. Ercole, Duke of Ferrara from 1471 to 1505, had two beautiful and talented daughters, Isabella and Beatrice, both of whom received a thorough classical education. Isabella (1474–1539) married Francesco Gonzago, Marquis of Mantua, and lived there for nearly half a century. For much of the time she acted as regent for her husband, a professional soldier or *condottiere*. In the process she became the greatest of all female collectors and patronesses of the Renaissance. Her *studiolo* – a combination of study and collector's cabinet of curiosities – became one of the finest in Italy. It was decorated by Andrea Mantegna, Pietro Perugino, Correggio and other major artists, and became so crowded with books and objets d'art – jewels, medals, small bronzes and marbles, pieces of amber, a 'unicorn's horn' and other natural curiosities – that she added onto it a 'grotto', one of the earliest instances of what remained a fey but often charming art form of the rich for the next 300 years. She owned a Michelangelo and a Jan van Eyck, and the inventory compiled after her death lists over 1600 items, from medals to stone vases.

An even more famous *studiolo* was constructed for Federigo da Montefeltro (1442–82), one of the great characters of the Renaissance, whose unmistakable profile, with its jutting nose, the bridge of which had been indented by a sword-blow, figures on many a Renaissance masterpiece. Like various other rulers of petty Italian states, he hired himself and his soldiers out for pay, and became one of the most successful of all the bloodstained *condottieri*, the outstanding master of what was then an honoured profession. His family had dominated Urbino since the thirteenth century, and he ran the city for nearly forty years, the last eight as duke. This millionaire mercenary had acquired a good knowledge of Latin and much other learning, together with excellent taste, and in his retirement from war he expiated his sins by a great deal of discerning patronage of the arts and even a little religious piety. He transformed the old medieval home of his ancestors in Urbino into one of the finest palaces in Italy, military in external appearance but with magnificent interiors in the latest taste. At the heart of it was his *studiolo*, a masterpiece of inlaid wood arranged as a series of *trompe-l'oeil* panels. There, the old warrior could converse with scholars and play the *uomo universale*.

Duke Federigo's court was a model of its times and it is no accident that when Baldassare Castiglione (1478–1529) decided to write a manual of courtly behaviour, which should be both a treatise on good manners at the highest level and a popularization of Renaissance ideals, he made Urbino the setting. *Il Cortigiano* *(The Courtier)* is a series of imaginary dialogues between experienced members of the duke's court, discussing and describing the ideal gentleman and gentlewoman and how they can be made fit for the best court society. The author, from Mantua, was well versed in the classics and had done court service not only at Urbino but under the Gonzagas in his home city, so he knew what he was writing about. When it was published in 1528 it won the approval of the authorities but, more important, it delighted young people and has remained a classic ever since, albeit little read these days. In its time it was a winner, and no book did more to turn the notions of the Renaissance elite into the received wisdom of Europe. To complete Castiglione's good fortune, he was made the subject of Raphael's finest surviving portrait.

However, while he was describing the sunny and elegant side of court life in the Renaissance, his contemporary Niccolò Machiavelli (1469–1527) was completing the picture with the darker and, it must be said, more realistic side. *Il Principe* *(The Prince)* was written in 1513, after Machiavelli, who had been involved in both the military and the diplomatic side of Florentine government, had been dismissed from office when the Medici returned to power in 1512. He was a historian as well as a man of the world, the author of books on Florentine history and the art of war. He was concerned not so much with ideals, as Castiglione purported to be, as with what actually happened in a rough and pitiless world. He told the reader: this is not what rulers ought to do, but what I know from my own experience they actually do, or try to do, in order to outwit their internal and external enemies. It is not, as its critics have maintained at the time and since, a diabolical book, designed to discourage the virtuous and to corrupt the ambitious. It is the original work of *realpolitik*, not without a certain resigned wisdom, and a patriotic work too, written from the viewpoint of a proud Florentine who had seen republican ideals and local freedoms ruined by invading armies, and recognized sadly that if the great cities of Italy were to survive as independent states they had to be ruled by shrewd men without illusions, who drew on the lessons of recent history.

Castiglione soothed and Machiavelli shocked, but both provided valuable information of a do-it-yourself kind, and no two treatises did more to spread all over Europe the hard-won knowledge of an Italy which, by the date they were published, had lived through a cultural revolution over a century old, and a series of invasions that were destroying her liberties and torturing her soul. They were key items in the Renaissance export trade. But of course, just as Italian towns were quick to swallow and assimilate the changes in the printing trade, and make them their own, so the rest of Europe was avid for Italian ideas and techniques, and had been so for the best part of two centuries.

Yet the speed at which Italian ideas radiated across Europe was determined to a great extent by historical accident as well as by the availability of talent. Initially at least, France was slow to respond, or appeared so. That was surprising. In the thirteenth century France, rather than Italy, seemed the cultural heart of Europe. Paris had by far the busiest university in the world, whose influence continued to grow as the century progressed. There were three major French-speaking courts, with Burgundy richer than the Kingdom of France in some respects, and Navarre also a francophone cultural centre of some importance. French as a language was maturing rapidly and in 1250 or even 1300 a poet was more likely to follow French verse-forms than Italian ones. Provence was also the theatre of a poetical movement, and from 1309 to 1378 one of its cities, Avignon, was the seat of the Vatican court during its 'Babylonian exile' from Rome, attracting men of letters and early humanists from all over the Latin West, including Petrarch, who occasionally wrote in French.

But France could produce no Dante, which was probably decisive in the battle of tongues. Moreover, southern France was ravaged by endemic outbreaks of militant heresy, and increasingly violent efforts to suppress them. From the 1330s it was the victim of periodic and devastating English invasions, in which Burgundy often joined, and from the 1420s onwards the French crown was engaged in a long and costly effort to recover its lost provinces from English occupation. In the second half of the fifteenth century France was acquiring the basis of its modern territorial composition, absorbing Gascony in 1453, Armagnac in 1473, Burgundy in 1477, Provence in 1481, Anjou in 1489 and Brittany in 1491. In the long run, this huge consolidation (followed by the annexation of Bourbon territory in 1527) was to make France the richest state in Europe by far. But at the time, the impact was absorbed by the consequences of Charles VIII's decision, in 1494, to pursue his claim to the Kingdom of Naples by invading Italy. This incursion, catastrophic for Italy, became a source of weakness for France too, for it was repeated by Charles's successors, Louis XII and François I, at great cost and to little effect, culminating in François' catastrophic defeat and capture at the Battle of Pavia (1525).

During the long decades of political and military preoccupations France was not, naturally, immune to the new Renaissance spirit. On the contrary: it was used to put a classical gloss on French expansionism. The French court was crowded with clever Italians, exiles from Florence and the papal court and from the faction-fighting in Genoa and Milan, egging on the Valois kings in the hope that a French conquest of Italy would reverse their own fallen fortunes. The heroic shades of antiquity were invoked by French propagandists. Charles and Louis were compared to Hannibal, crossing the Alps. François was presented as conducting a dialogue with Julius Caesar (an Italian who had reversed the conquest by invading Gaul). This work was accompanied by Caesar's *Commentaries*, in a version exquisitely illuminated by Albert Pigghe and Godefroy le Batave, which must rank as one of the finest of all Renaissance manuscripts and is among the great treasures of the Bibliothèque Nationale. The invasions were also celebrated in medallions, enamels, statues, triumphal arches and prints, all in classical mode and often with the help of Italian craftsmen. But the great French Renaissance writer was slow to appear. François Villon (1431–65?), the only outstanding fifteenth-century French poet, was curiously untouched by the Renaissance, and in the mere 3,000 lines of his verses that have survived it is hard to find traces of the new spirit – he is the Middle Ages in all their brutal magnificence.

However, in the long run the Renaissance struck France with shattering force. Charles VIII returned from Italy with a score of expert workmen, but it was François I who embraced the new culture enthusiastically on behalf of his country. He was employing Leonardo da Vinci in France as early as 1516, and he likewise brought over artists of the stature of Primaticcio and Giovanni Battista Rosso. These men worked alongside French artists like Jean Goujon and Jean Cousin to form the École de Fontainebleau, the first major Renaissance artistic centre outside Italy. François carried through, with Italian assistance and inspiration, what is probably the largest programme of chateaux or palace building in history, mainly in the Loire valley.

Equally important was the French passion for Renaissance writings. This too came late, but once the Sorbonne set up its own press in 1470, French editions and translations of the classics began to appear in large numbers. Robert Gaguin (1433–1501) struck a popular Gallic note by combining Renaissance studies with the burgeoning French nationalism that marked the second half of the fifteenth century. He published his *Compendium supra Francorum gestis* (1497), a Latin history of France up to the present, taught rhetoric at Paris and produced a treatise on how to enjoy and write Latin verse. He was joined by Guillaume Fichet and Lefèvre d'Étaples, who toured Italy to pick up the latest scholarship, and by Greek teachers such as Heronymus and Lascaris. Even more influential was Guillaume Budé (1468–1540), who in 1532 published *The Right and Proper Institution of the Study of Learning*. His theme was that Christendom, itself perfect when pristine, had been buried in 'centuries of barbarism', and it was the task of the present age to 'reform the choirs of the antique muses'. The church did not exactly relish this approach, so many of its institutions being associated, in humanist eyes, with the barbarous centuries. Hence when Budé persuaded François I to subsidize the new humanist culture, by founding chairs of Latin, Greek, Hebrew and Arabic, they were grouped in what was called the Collège Royal (later, the Collège de France) outside the control of Paris University. This was the point at which the French literary Renaissance matured, one might almost say exploded.

Some writers, such as François Rabelais (1494–1553), were educated in the old manner. An ordained priest, he is believed to have attended the ultra-strict Collège de Mont Aigu of the University of Paris, notorious for its stink, its floggings and bad food, and known as 'the cleft between the buttocks of Mother Church'. Like Erasmus, who also attended it, he was unhappy there, though it must be said that other alumni – Jean Calvin, the great heresiarch, and Ignatius Loyola, founder of the Jesuits – glorified its teaching, but these judgments tell us as much about the temperaments of the four men as about the institution. Rabelais qualified as a doctor. This was an area where French studies had been revolutionized by contacts and experience during the Italian campaigns. Ambroise Paré (1510–90), who served in one of them, went on to become perhaps the greatest physiologist of the age. He settled in Lyons, a town colonized by Italian bankers – on François I's death it was said that the crown owed twice its annual income to the Lyons bankers – who brought with them the trappings of the Italian Renaissance. Rabelais wrote extensively in Latin and French on a variety of subjects, including medicine, but it is his serio-comic masterpiece, published over twenty years in five parts but usually known as *Gargantua and Pantagruel*, a compendium of humanism, bawdy, satire and description, that made its way into French hearts. He covered almost every aspect of French society, from peasants to academics, from merchants and lawyers to courtiers, and he wrote vivid, terse, expressive and powerful French, with an enormous vocabulary, using dialect, slang and neologisms. It would be going too far to say he invented French as a literary language, as Dante had invented Italian. Rather, he demonstrated its enormous potentialities, and made the French excited about their linguistic heritage for the first time. The church condemned him; civil authorities ordered his books to be prosecuted and burned; the Sorbonne was unremittingly hostile. But the court and the literate people loved both the fun and the savage criticisms of society, and the huge, untidy book served as inspiration to writers as diverse as Molière and Voltaire, besides becoming a byword for iniquity throughout the Anglo-Saxon and northern European world.

Younger writers benefited from the educational reforms carried out by Budé with François I's blessing. Jean Dorat, first professor of Greek at the new college, numbered among his pupils Joachim du Bellay (1522–60), who sought to marry knowledge of the classics with the newly mature national tongue and who published, in 1549, the first key work of philology, *Defence and Illustration of the French Language*, a plea for French poets to write odes and elegies adapted from the classics, and to use the new form of the Petrarchan sonnet. His fellow student, Pierre de Ronsard (1524–85), published his first odes the following year, and the two men, together with their colleague Jean-Antoine de Baif (1532–89), who had been born in Venice, the son of the French ambassador, and had absorbed humanism from infancy, constituted a constellation of 'new' poets known as the Pléiade. They set the rules for French poetry for nearly three centuries, but they also influenced the drama, for another member of the Pléiade, Étienne Jodelle (1531–88), wrote an epoch-making play, *Dido's Self-sacrifice*, which became the exemplar of French classic theatre, thus setting the scene for the glories of the seventeenth century.

These lively spirits created a language that writers could play with indefinitely and in myriad forms. One of the most enduring was the essay, which lives on today in the critical article and the newspaper and magazine feature. Michel de Montaigne (1533–92) was the outstanding product of French humanism, and is still read today all over the world. He was well born, well read, experienced in administration but sufficiently *désabusé* by the world to devote himself chiefly to letters, which took the form of informal reflections on men, events, customs and beliefs, and the common milestones of life – birth, youth, manhood, marriage, sickness and death. He was a Catholic, but a sceptic; a practical man but a man of acute feeling too; one who loved the past but was at home in the present and feared not the future. For the first time in European literature, we catch the modern tone, which is easy and conversational, and the willingness to talk about oneself to the reader. The publication of his *Essais* in 1580 marked the immense distance that the forces of Reformation humanism had now carried the world since the Middle Ages began to wane.

The distance travelled in England was equally great but the route was different. The English language began its own battle for self-discovery at almost the same time as Italian, in the early fourteenth century, when the use of French by the ruling class, at court, in the law and in administration, was finally replaced by the demotic tongue, English, a process given legal force by the Statute of Pleadings. The Hundred Years War with France completed the bifurcation, and it is significant that its early stages coincided with the development of England's first independent style of Gothic architecture, the Perpendicular. Its first masterpiece was Gloucester Abbey, where the entire east end was rebuilt in the new style, crowned with a giant east window, the largest in England, to celebrate the great English victory over France at Crécy (1346).

At about this time was born Geoffrey Chaucer, who was to become the greatest poet of the Middle Ages, after Dante himself; and, like Dante, to adumbrate the salient characteristics of Renaissance literature. He came from a family of Ipswich vintners, who traded with Spain, France and Portugal, and like many vintners' sons (John Ruskin was another example) developed early a wide international outlook, especially in cultural matters. A spell as page to Lionel, one of Edward III's sons, introduced him to court life. He served in one of the king's invading armies in France – a country he visited often – and he then joined Edward's household, the king using him as a diplomatic envoy more than once. Thus he went to Genoa, and again to Flanders, and in 1378 he was in Lombardy as part of a mission negotiating with Bernabò Visconti and the great *condottiere* Sir John Hawkwood 'for certain affairs touching the expedition of the King's war'.

Chaucer had already produced a version of the French *Roman de la Rose* and had written poetry on his own account. By learning Italian he opened up for himself the new world of Dante, Boccaccio and Petrarch, to each of whom, but especially the second, he was indebted. Even when not abroad he kept in touch with the Continent by virtue of his splendid job as Controller of the Customs on wool, hides and skins at London port. A series of major poems followed, with Boccaccio as his model and supplier of ideas. But Chaucer was entirely his own man, and very much an Englishman. Indeed, he was an important Englishman, becoming clerk of the King's Works, and thus in charge of the fabric of the Tower of London, Westminster Palace and eight other royal houses, as well as being Justice of the Peace and MP for Kent. He thus fitted into the developing Renaissance pattern of the courtly man of affairs who practised the art of poetry.

He also shared the Renaissance fascination with the individual human being, as opposed to the archetype or mere category. The individual dominates his masterpiece, *The Canterbury Tales*, which he wrote between 1386, when he went into semi-retirement in Kent, and his death in 1400. The work has no precise model, for Chaucer had not read the *Decameron*, and the framework of a Canterbury pilgrimage to the famous shrine of St Thomas à Becket, with each member of a brilliantly varied company telling a tale, is entirely Chaucer's. More important is the vivid directness with which Chaucer brings out character, both in describing his pilgrims and within the tales they tell. It is the literary equivalent of the discovery of the laws of perspective and foreshortening by the artists of Florence. These men and women jump out from the pages, and live on in the memory, in ways that not even Dante could contrive. There is genius here, of an inexplicable kind: Chaucer is one of the four English writers – the other three being Shakespeare, Dickens and Kipling – whose extraordinary ability to peer into the mind of diverse human creatures defies rational explanation and can only be attributed to a mysterious *daemon*. It is odd that English literature should have suddenly exploded with such a magician.

But then, that is the nature of culture. We can give all kinds of satisfying explanations of why and when the Renaissance occurred and how it transmitted itself. But there is no explaining Dante, no explaining Chaucer. Genius suddenly comes to life, and speaks out of a vacuum. Then it is silent, equally mysteriously. The trends continue and intensify, but genius is lacking. Chaucer had no successor of anything approaching similar stature. There is no major poet in fifteenth-century English literature. But the page is not blank. Quite the contrary: there was much solid progress in creating the infrastructure of scholarship and letters. Henry V, greatest of the Plantagenet monarchs, and conqueror of France, died young in 1422. His son, Henry VI, was one year old, and the regency fell to his uncle, Humphrey, Duke of Gloucester. Duke Humphrey was a poor ruler, and thus began the weakness and misjudgments that led to the loss of France and the Wars of the Roses. But he was the first English patron of Renaissance learning. He collected the Greek and Latin classics, including most of Aristotle and Plato, in fine manuscripts, and beautifully illustrated editions of modern masters, including Dante, Petrarch and Boccaccio. He bequeathed them all to Oxford University, where they became the nucleus of the future Bodleian Library – indeed, 'Duke Humphrey' is still the physical and antiquarian core of the entire institution. In Chaucer's time, William of Wykeham, Bishop of Winchester, had begun the process of translating England's new-found wealth, based mainly on wool, into scholarly stones, with his twin foundations of Winchester College and New College, Oxford. Henry VI, a hopeless king but a pious and generous man, continued it with Eton College and King's College, Cambridge. Other colleges followed in stately procession, including All Souls at Oxford, which was to become the English equivalent of the Collège de France, and St John's, Cambridge, which from the start specialized in studies dear to Renaissance man.

The first outstanding English humanist, Robert Flemmyng, visited Italy, where he formed connections at the court of Sixtus IV, the learned pope, and won the friendship of his famous librarian, Platina. To go to Italy became the form. Thomas Linacre (1460–1524) went there to sit at the feet of Politian, alongside Giovanni de' Medici, later Pope Leo X. Linacre took a medical degree at Padua and came back to found the College of Physicians, write a Latin grammar and act as tutor to royal children. His friend William Grocyn (1449–1519) also studied under Politian, and the even more learned Greek scholar Chalcondyles. When he returned, he delivered the first public lecture on Greek at Oxford

(1491). Desiderius Erasmus (1467–1536), Thomas More (1477–1535) and John Colet (1466–1519) all studied under Grocyn, Erasmus coming to Oxford in 1498 because, he said, it was no longer necessary to go as far as Italy to pick up the latest in Greek scholarship – Oxford could provide as good or better.

One feature of English scholarship, both at Oxford and Cambridge, was its spirit of criticism. This is an immensely important point, and is worth dwelling on a little. Of course the critical spirit – that is, the tendency not simply to accept texts at their face value but to examine their provenance, credentials, authenticity and contents with a wary eye – was not invented in Oxford. It was a Renaissance characteristic, and one that was to prove fatal to the unity of the church, once it was applied to sacred texts and ecclesiastical credentials. It long antedated the Renaissance, needless to say. Indeed, it went back to Marcion, in the second century AD, who first subjected the canonical texts of the New Testament to careful exegesis, accepting some and rejecting others. But this kind of approach was rare in the Dark and even in the Middle Ages; it is odd that churchmen-scholars of the calibre of St Augustine or Thomas Aquinas paid so little attention to the integrity and background of the texts that came down to them, and on which they commented so copiously. But so it was. Thus the revival of the sceptical approach of Marcion was one of the most striking aspects of the recovery of antiquity, and the most explosive.

The trail was blazed by Lorenzo Valla (1406–57), a clever, difficult, quarrelsome but also painstaking and exact scholar, who specialized in rhetoric, and lectured on it in Padua, Rome and Naples. He was a man of affairs, both at the papal court and under Alfonso of Aragon, King of Naples. In the periodic struggles between the secular and ecclesiastical forces, he tended to sympathize with princes rather than popes. This led him to examine critically the Donation of Constantine. This document was fabricated sometime between 750 and 850 AD and purported to be a record of the conversion of the Emperor Constantine, and the various principalities he conferred on the then pope, Sylvester I (314–35), and all his successors. It made him primate over all the other Christian churches, with secular dominion over Rome 'and all the provinces, places and *civitates* of Italy and the Western Regions, and supreme judge of their clergy everywhere'. It records that Sylvester was even offered the imperial crown of the West, but refused it. The Donation was the Ur-text of papal triumphalism, the chief credential for the Hildebrandine revolution of the eleventh century and of the even more extreme statement of claim by Boniface VIII in the fourteenth century, as well as the title deeds to the lands of the papal states in Italy. It had been challenged before, more as a gesture of political defiance by aggrieved monarchs than in a spirit of scholarship. But Valla subjected it to textual scrutiny based upon the principles of what was to become modern historical criticism, and showed, beyond any reasonable doubt, that it was a deliberate forgery. He presented his findings in *De Falso Credita et Ementita Constantini Donatione Declamatio* (1440). Valla had already been in trouble with the church authorities over his criticism of the dialectical teaching techniques of church scholars, especially friars, at the universities. As his exposure of the forgery also went on to make a frontal attack on the temporal power of the papacy, which he argued should be a spiritual institution solely, he was summoned before the Inquisition (1444) and only saved by the intervention of King Alfonso.

It is not surprising that Valla fell foul of the church, for his approach to all ancient documents was that nothing was sacred, and all ought to be examined by the light of a powerful critical candle. He undertook a comparison between St Jerome's Latin Vulgate (Bible translation) and the Greek New Testament. This was not only important in itself and later had a major influence on Erasmus's textual criticism, but encouraged other scholars to do the same, over a whole range of texts. Thus in 1497, John Colet, who had been in Italy for the last four years, gathering information about how to examine ancient texts, gave a sensational and historic series of Oxford lectures on St Paul's Epistle to the Romans. He abandoned the scholastic approach altogether, and instead placed the Epistle, one of the most central of all Christian documents since it includes the theology of justification by faith, against its Roman historical background, using pagan authorities like Suetonius. This new historical approach was electrifying for clever young men. It was fresh, catchy, irreverent, iconoclastic and immensely appealing. It was one of those *omnium gatherum* revolutions in understanding (as was, later, Marx's class analysis of history or Freud's theory of the unconscious), which could be made to apply to all kinds of things and problems, with startling results.

What was developing, in short, was the first great cultural war in European history. One has a vivid glimpse of the future when, some time between 1511 and 1513, Erasmus and John Colet visited together the famous shrine of St Thomas in Canterbury. This rivalled in wealth and fame the shrine of St James in Compostela and was surrounded by rackets and fake marvels of all kinds. The two scholars were revolted by what they saw, especially the riches, which Colet said angrily should be given to the poor. He refused to bestow a reverential kiss on a prize relic, the 'Arm of St George', dismissed a rag supposedly dipped in St Thomas's blood 'with a whistle of contempt' and exploded when a licensed beggar showered him with holy water and offered him St Thomas's shoe to be kissed. He said to Erasmus: 'Do these fools expect us to kiss the shoe of every good man who ever lived? Why not bring us their spittle or their dung to be kissed?' It was more than a hundred years since Chaucer's pilgrims had come to Canterbury, 'the holy blissful martyr for to seke', full of unquestioned faith in his miracle-making capacities. In the meantime the Renaissance had been doing its work. Medieval certitude – or credulity depending on your viewpoint – was now faced with Renaissance scrutiny, or scepticism.

With the benefit of hindsight it seems strange that the church did not see what was coming and take steps to prepare for or even resist it. In German-speaking central Europe the culture war was clearly stirring by the second half of the fifteenth century, with books pouring from the presses in ever-growing number and quantity. In the half century up to 1500, nearly 25,000 works were printed in Germany, and given the average edition-size of 250, that means six million printed books were circulating in Germany alone. Most of the German humanists were men grown critical of the church. The archetypal one, Ulrich von Hutten (1488–1523), a poet awarded the laureate by the Emperor Maximilian, attacked, among other things, the old-style teaching at Cologne University (he had attended no less than seven universities himself, including Bologna where he learned Greek), the sale of indulgences, the useless life of monks, corruption in Rome and the trade in relics. Significantly, he brought out a new edition of Valla's book on the Donation of Constantine. Hutten wrote a fluent new kind of German, witty, pithy and full of popular expressions, and with it went a new kind of nationalism which, north of the Alps, was one of the products of the Renaissance turmoil. Indeed, he was a Renaissance man through and through – even his death was the doing of the new Renaissance scourge, syphilis. He pronounced Latin in the new, scholarly way, denouncing the church for its 'barbarous' usage, and he took pride in his 'correct' pronunciation of classical Greek, another point on which the church fell short. Indeed, pronunciation of Latin and Greek was an infallible test of which side you were on in the culture war. Like other humanists, Hutten sought protection from the secular power when the church authorities moved against him, and got it. This was a growing pattern as the Renaissance progressed.

Even in Spain, land of the last great crusader people, which finally 'purified' itself in the 1490s by expelling Moslems and Jews, the church seemed unaware of the danger to itself that the new progressive forces of Renaissance scholarship embodied. Spain was emerging as a major Mediterranean power, indeed an Italian power too, absorbing the Balearic Islands, Sardinia, Sicily and Naples, even before the accession of Charles I of Spain in 1516, and his election as Charles V of the Holy Roman Empire in 1519, created the largest agglomeration of power in Europe, and the world. Throughout the fifteenth century, Spanish contacts with the Italy of the Renaissance grew, and not only the courts and chanceries but the archbishops' palaces (as in Saragossa) became centres of humanist learning, where the classics of antiquity were translated and, from the 1470s, printed. It is significant that the troublesome Lorenzo Valla wrote the life of the father of Alfonso V ('The Magnanimous'), King of Aragon, who spent much of his life, 1416–58, absorbing the new culture in his Italian territories. When Ferdinand of Aragon and Isabella of Castile united the crowns, they gave their joint support to the propagation of humanist scholarship throughout Spain. It was with the personal encouragement of Isabella that the most vigorous of the Italian-trained Spanish humanists, Antonio de Nebrija (1444–1522), waged fire and sword against the old teaching at Salamanca, Spain's oldest and finest university. He called himself a *conquistador* and his enemy 'barbarism'. He replaced the old-style Latin manuals used at Salamanca and elsewhere with his new book *Introductions to Latin* (1481), dedicated to Isabella, and translated and circulated all over Europe.

The 'Catholic Monarchs', as Ferdinand and Isabella were known, were impelled in a humanist direction not only by their own tastes but by the advice of their great primate, the Cardinal-Archbishop of Toledo, Francisco Jimenez de Cisneros (1436–1517). It was he who in 1509 founded at Alcala de Henares the Complutensian University (using the Latin place-name of Alcala) for the study of Hebrew, Greek and Latin and the training of priests in the new humanist methods. This in turn gave birth to the great Complutensian Polyglot Bible, first printed in 1514–17. He was a patron of Erasmus, and anxious that he should come to Spain to teach. The Low Countries connection was strengthened after 1516, when Charles's Habsburg territories there were united with the Spanish crown. The Spanish humanists delighted in Erasmian satire, their favourite being his *In Praise of Folly*, a book that had a profound influence on Miguel de Cervantes (1547–1616), Spain's first great writer of world stature, whose novel *Don Quixote* is both the last word on the vanished world of medieval chivalry and the first to tackle the pathos of modern life.

If Erasmus was the hero of the Spanish humanists, his own hero, insofar as he had one, was Valla. He wrote: 'In me you see the avenger of Valla's wrongs. I have undertaken to defend his scholarship, the most distinguished I know. Never shall I allow that scholarship to be attacked or destroyed with impunity because of anyone's insolence.' He particularly championed Valla's *Elegantiarum Latinae Linguae*, a manual for writers in Latin, which set new standards of excellence. More than fifty manuscripts of this work and 150 early printed editions survive, which indicates its wide circulation and popularity. In 1489 Erasmus, while still a student, wrote a shortened version of it and he produced another digest for publication in 1498; this went into at least fifty editions. It is notable that both Valla and Erasmus referred to their opponents as 'barbarians', and it is a melancholy fact that, as humanism spread, especially in northern Europe, its language became more vituperative, provoking in turn harsh language from those thus classified, who held the leading positions in the church. Thus the culture war intensified itself and became more vicious. We have dealt so far with its open, literary expression in manuscripts and printed books. It is now time to turn to its mute but visible images, in bronze and stone, paint and plaster, bricks and mortar.

PART THREE

The Anatomy of Renaissance Sculpture

Rarely in human history have the visual arts enjoyed such an intense and prolonged period of splendour as during the Renaissance. The riches are almost infinite indeed, and describing them presents special problems. A purely chronological approach is tedious and often unenlightening. On the other hand to treat them by categories – sculpture, painting, architecture – overrides the fact that individual artists often crossed these boundaries, and most of them emerged from studios that practised many of the arts. However, provided we bear this in mind, the categorical treatment is clearer, and it is right to begin with sculpture, for the Renaissance was concerned with the presentation of human reality, and sculpture with its three-dimensional evocation of human figures is the most direct in achieving this end.

The story of Renaissance sculpture begins with Nicola Pisano, who lived approximately between 1220 and 1284. He came from Apulia in the heel of Italy but most of his working life was spent in Pisa, Bologna, Siena, Perugia and other central Italian towns. He was a product of the brilliant if precarious court culture created by the Emperor Frederick II, known as *stupor mundi* or 'the Wonder of the World'. Frederick built palatial castles in southern Italy, patronized artists and craftsmen of all kinds, imported ideas and technology from the eastern Mediterranean and the Orient and, not least, sought to revive classical forms. Pisano was clearly trained in one of the emperor's south Italian workshops, and he brought to Tuscany something new: the classical anxiety to represent the human body accurately, to show emotions not symbolically but as they are actually seen on human faces, to distinguish with infinite gradations between youth and age, and to render men and women as living, breathing, individual creatures.

Nicola Pisano was, by any chronological criterion, a medieval artist. His first recorded work, the pulpit in the Pisa Baptistery

(1260), was carved two years after the Sainte-Chapelle in Paris was complete and work was just beginning on Cologne Cathedral and the cloister of Westminster Abbey. But his spirit was already post-medieval. The marble reliefs in the Pisan pulpit show real human beings with faces full of care and anxiety, each a portrait. Pisano incorporates in his work the achievements of French Gothic sculpture, but his figures, fresh with life, are a whole epoch away from the elongated saints and angels on the west front of Chartres Cathedral, beautiful though they are, which remain symbolic and inanimate by comparison. Pisano's *Last Judgment*, in marble relief from his pulpit in Siena Cathedral, from the late 1260s, is a medieval scene in conception, with ferocious devils torturing the damned. But the execution carries faint echoes of classical Greece: the embodied souls, whether saved or damned, emerge as individuals, not types; they have faces you would see in the Sienese streets, and bodies you can imagine walking or running – real, working bodies. Nicola's son Giovanni Pisano (c. 1245–1319) pushed this humanizing process further: he has, for instance, three marble figures in the Arena Chapel in Padua (c. 1305) which might almost have sprung from the Acropolis in Athens.

Already, by this date, Italians with a scholarly and antiquarian taste were poking about among the ruins of ancient Rome and other cities, which were much more extensive in medieval times than they are now, studying inscriptions, collecting medals and coins with low-relief heads, and handling bits of broken sculpture to be found in the debris. Artists were often among those foraging parties, looking not just for the forms of antiquity but the technology that produced them. From this time there was a revival of casting in bronze for artistic purposes. The technique had not been lost but it had been used, in the Dark and Middle Ages, mainly by bell-foundries. When Andrea Pisano (c. 1295–1349), not related to Nicola and his son, created a series of bronze reliefs for the doors of the south portal of the Baptistery at Florence, in 1330, he merely modelled them in wax. They then had to be cast by the Venetian bell-founder Leonardo Avanzi and his team. Thereafter, however, the success of bronze low-reliefs led artistic workshops to set up their own foundries.

Andrea Pisano began his professional life as a goldsmith, as did most of the early sculptors in bronze. By the end of the fourteenth century, an artist-craftsman in a busy workshop, especially in Florence which was already emerging as the richest and most art-conscious of the Italian towns, expected to work on almost every kind of stone, from limestone and Carrara marble, to semi-precious and precious stones, and to deal with heated metals, ranging from gold to copper, and copper-alloys such as bronze, which had a mixture of tin. Goldsmiths played a much more central role in Renaissance art than is generally realized. Their skills were absorbed by the sculptors and their designs by the painters. The rich in Florence and other commercial cities liked to flaunt their wealth. They probably spent more on jewellery than on art, and one of the functions of the painters was to record in exact and realistic detail the jewels worn by their sitters, male and female – the brilliant depiction of jewellery was a skill that any Renaissance portrait-painter had to possess. Bronze doors, with superb panels depicting scenes from the Old and New Testaments, were the outstanding way in which the art of the jeweller could be transferred to the adorning of a new cathedral in hard-edged and permanent form. The frames and surrounds in which the illustrative panels are placed are essentially jewel-settings.

Hence the importance that the Florentines, and the artists who served them, attached to the bronze doors of their cathedral and its related buildings; these increasingly elaborate artefacts were the jewels of God's house, set in it for eternity. Immense care and years of work were devoted to them. This had important consequences. Even in the thirteenth century, commercially minded towns commissioning artists to do elaborate work insisted on detailed and binding contracts. Nicola Pisano, in order to get the commission to make the pulpit in Siena Cathedral, had to sign a contract, which survives, dated 29 September 1265, setting down what he had promised to do in meticulous manner, what materials he had to use and what time he had to spend on the site. These contracts had the effect of identifying the artist in a way that had hitherto been very rare – it plucked him forth from the mass of anonymous craftsmen and made him famous, or conscious of fame. Sculptors and painters began to sign their work. Thus the reliefs on the Florence Baptistery doors are signed 'Andreas Ugolino Nini de Pisis Me Fecit'. The emergence of the artist as an individual coincided with the emergence of the individual in his works – both processes reinforced each other.

It was another consequence of Italian urban commercialism that patrons, conscious that their increased expenditure on art was drawing more and more gifted young men into the business, began to spur them on by holding public competitions for major contracts. At the end of the fourteenth century, Florence was enjoying a period of peace, prosperity and civic pride, and its elders decided to commission a second Baptistery door. Andrea Pisano's doors were the standard of excellence against which the new generation of sculptors were to be judged. The ensuing competition of 1401 has often been treated as the single event that marked the real onset of the Florentine Renaissance. It was certainly a remarkable occasion. There were thirty-four judges, drawn not just from the cathedral authorities but from the city guilds and from surrounding towns. They advertised the contest all over Italy, and masters or would-be masters arrived from the entire peninsula. The field was narrowed down to seven, including three of the greatest artists of the entire period: Filippo Brunelleschi (1377–1446), Jacopo della Quercia (1374–1438) and Lorenzo Ghiberti (1378–1455). Each of those shortlisted was given four sheets of bronze and told to conceive a design to illustrate 'The Sacrifice of Isaac'.

Only two of the designs, by Brunelleschi and Ghiberti, have survived, and the judges had a hard task deciding between them. In fact they took two years to make up their minds, conscious of the size of the project and the enormity of the expense. (The eventual cost was 22,000 florins, equal to the entire defence budget of the city of Florence.) Ghiberti got the contract, probably because the judges thought he was the man most likely to carry through the job to a triumphant conclusion. And they were right. As Ghiberti boasts in his *Autobiography*, he put art before 'the chase after lucre'. He was astonishingly conscientious and an obsessional perfectionist. He appears to us a very slow worker, but one has to bear in mind that the standards of craftsmanship demanded and provided in late medieval and early Renaissance times were of a quality inconceivable to the modern age, and speed of execution was not possible. Ghiberti would spend years on a single piece of jewellery or a tombstone, months on hand-chasing a piece of bronze. Three years was normal for him in creating a large marble statue.

Ghiberti was a young man in 1403 when he started on the bronze doors, completing the original contract twenty years later. He was then given a further commission to decorate a third set of doors, later known as the Gates of Paradise. He finished them in 1452, three years before his death. So he spent virtually his entire working life, over half a century, on these Florentine doors. He had many gifted assistants, including Donatello (1386–1466), Benozzo Gozzoli (1420–97), Paolo Uccello (1397–1475), Antonio Pollaiuolo (1431–98) and perhaps Luca della Robbia (1399–1482), so that his workshop was one of the great creative furnaces of the Renaissance. But he himself was the artist-creator down to the last micromillimetre. As Ghiberti himself claimed, this cumulatively huge work (his first door alone carried twenty-eight panels, which with borders weighed 34,000 pounds) was executed 'with much care and industry . . . understanding and artifice'. The state of the art was such that some castings failed and had to be done again, and even the successful casts required finishing, which in some cases took years. Ghiberti's doors, recreating the scriptures in dramatic life, were the cynosure of artists and collectors from all over Italy, who came to admire and learn. They summed up everything the Renaissance had accomplished so far, and marked the way ahead for younger artists.

The sculptor who absorbed Ghiberti's lessons most productively, and built on his work most confidently, was Donatello. His life and work tell us a great deal about the Renaissance, what it was and what it was not. The ideas behind the Renaissance, particularly the overwhelming desire, in letters, to get at the truth and, in art, to present the truth as we see it, were a force that pushed writers and artists to the highest levels. But the Renaissance was not determinative. Artists, in particular, were not forced to conform to its aims by its compulsive spirit. Rather, it gave artists much greater opportunities than in medieval times to be themselves and develop their capacities to the full. Hence it unleashed the geniuses. And there was no man who possessed genius so obviously and persistently as Donato di Niccolo di Betto Bardi, who was born in Florence in 1386 and died there eighty years later. Donatello was one of the greatest artists who ever lived and in some ways the central figure of the Renaissance. Before him, artists were aware of definite limits to what could or ought to be done in art. Donatello was so consistently and shockingly original that, after him, all the limits seemed to have disappeared, so that an artist was constrained only by his powers.

He was the son of a humble woodcarver and remained, all his life, a man who worked with his hands. Unlike many successful Renaissance artists, such as Ghiberti, to whom he was apprenticed 1404–7, Donatello had no social pretensions, no aesthetic pride, no swagger. He spoke and lived in a rough way, like the craftsman he was. Patrons sometimes gave him fine suits of clothes, which they thought befitted his status as a great artist. He wore them once or twice, then discarded them. He never made much money, and in his old age, he lived on a pension from Cosimo de' Medici, who worshipped him. He does not seem to have accepted the fact that artists could now move in the best society and were becoming highly prized individuals, famous men. He was not interested. To that extent, one of the central facts of the Renaissance, the emergence of the artist-celebrity, left him unimpressed.

On the other hand, Donatello possessed artistic integrity to an unusual degree. He was unbiddable. His sense of honour, as a craftsman-artist, was overwhelming. He would do what he thought right, at his own pace, in his own way. Princes and cardinals did not impress him. Plebeian he was, but he spoke to them, on artistic matters, as an equal, indeed as a master. Like Ghiberti he was a perfectionist and would sometimes take years to get something absolutely right. He was not to be hurried, and if bullied would down tools. His name figures in hundreds of documents and many stories circulated about his rude sayings, rough humour, obduracy and unwillingness to take orders. His patrons, to their credit, respected him. One reason why the Renaissance produced so many marvellous works of art is that a high proportion of great and rich men were willing to respect artists who knew their minds and their worth. Here, Donatello led the way in educating the elite to a true spirit of cooperation with artists, so that by a paradox he, the obstinate plebeian, played a historic role in raising the social status of the producer of beauty, from craftsman to artist. After Donatello, there was no turning back: in Florence first, soon in all Italy, the artist was a man who commanded not only respect but attention, reverence, admiration and honour.

Donatello's technical accomplishments were spectacular. He could work in anything: stucco, wax, finished bronze (though he did not do his own casting), clay, marble, every kind of stone from the softest to the hardest, glass and wood. He used paint and gilt when he wished. He did not follow the rules of any particular technique but improvised when he wanted and used anything that came to hand to achieve new effects. To create the *Madonna dei Cordai* (Florence, Museo Bardini) he carved the Madonna and Child out of wood, like a jigsaw, covered it in setting material, placed it on a flat background over which he put a mosaic of gilt leather, then painted everything, with a final layer of varnish to bind it together. This artistic technique of sucking in materials to suit specific purposes, as the creative mind arbitrarily chooses, is what the French were later – nearly half a millennium later – to call *bricolage*. Such spontaneity was staggering in the first half of the fifteenth century. But Donatello was also capable of a carefully planned and deliberative extension of the frontiers of existing techniques: he invented, for instance, a delicate form of low-relief carving, *rilievo schiacciato*, which is not far from drawing. Slow and conscientious he was, when required, but few artists moved more easily and confidently among their materials.

Hence his constant originality. He was always doing things that had not been done before. Even before him, artists were moving away from the collectivist presentation of human beings that was so characteristic of medieval art, portraying them as individuals even in the high-relief of bronze or stone, and then going further and picking them out of the background into singular prominence. But it was Donatello who, as it were, once and for all, put individual humans on their own feet, as they had stood in ancient times, as separate statues. This involved a good deal of technical innovation, for instance to prevent statues from falling over, and –

a typical Renaissance touch, this – the application of scientific principles to visual presentation. Here are a dozen ways in which Donatello innovated.

First, his earliest masterpiece, *St John the Evangelist* done in 1408 for the great western portal of Florence Cathedral (now in the Duomo Museum), was worked with deliberately distorted proportions so that, seen directly in photos, it looks unstable and over-elongated; but when you get underneath it, to the position from which Donatello designed it to be seen, it looks over-whelmingly solid and powerful. No one had done this so con-vincingly before. Second, Donatello used ancient patterns to give weight and authority to his statues, an early example, 1411–13, being his marble *St Mark* in the Drapers' niche on Orsanmichele, Florence, a truly Renaissance figure compared to Ghiberti's nearby work, which still looks medieval.

Third, he made a statue live: thus the humanity of *St George*, carved in stone for the Guild of Armourers' niche on Orsan-michele (now in the Bargello), seems to come through the armour – his face and hands are alive, and he balances himself on the balls of his feet. As Vasari later observed: 'There is a wonderful suggestion of life bursting out of the stone.' Fourth, with the assistance of Michelozzo, an expert at casting, Donatello gave an object lesson in the potentialities of bronze with a *St Louis of Toulouse* (1418–22, now in the Museo dell' Opera di Santa Croce, Florence), with the mitre, gloves and crozier cast separately, and the magnificent cope cast in different sections, allowing the sculp-tor to display his virtuosity to the full. The same kind of innov-ation emerges in his *Jeremiah and Habakkuk* done for Giotto's campanile (1415 ff., Museo dell' Opera del Duomo), which uses experimental techniques to suit the settings and produces strik-ingly lively prophets, whom Donatello might have observed in the streets below. Liveliness is also the secret of a sixth innovation, a revival of the Roman bust, which he combined with the medieval practice of putting heads on containers for facial relics. But Donatello's heads appear to be of living men, even when they are done from death-masks. An exceptionally fine one is the terracotta bust of Nicolò da Uzzano (Bargello), one of the earliest true por-traits in the history of European art, yet another innovation.

An eighth innovation was the first 'humanist' tomb, of the anti-
pope John XXIII, done for the Florence Baptistery sometime after
1419. The effigy was cast, then gilded, and is an integral part of
an architectural setting, with a bier, sarcophagus, sorrowing Virgin
and other accessories (Michelozzo being the co-artist), an ensemble that became the pattern for many more, right up to the end of
the eighteenth century, in Canova's prime. Donatello used
complex decorative surrounds for the first time, for narrative
reliefs in his new *relievo schiacciato*, as in the beautiful *Christ
Giving the Keys to St Peter* (now in the Victoria and Albert
Museum). A tenth innovation, here and elsewhere, is the use of a
new kind of aerial perspective. Sometimes he employed stratified
marble for clouds. Sometimes he placed ruler and set-square in
damp stucco, then cut back the material with a spatula to suggest
receding planes. *The Feast of Herod* (now in Lille Museum), made
for the font in the Siena Cathedral Baptistery, is another excellent
example of the way Donatello used architecture to offset low-
relief, and vice versa, as in the singing gallery of Florence Cathedral, an ecstatic dance of the souls of the innocent in Paradise.

Donatello was always discovering new forms of art, and illuminating them with new tricks of the trade (as he would put it).
Thus the four evangelists in roundels in the old sacristy of San
Lorenzo, Florence, are real, lifelike old men, not prototype saints.
Equally innovative are the four roundels in the sacristy that deal
with the life of St John the Evangelist, many of the figures in
which are shown only in part, cut off by the frame of the roundel,
to give immediacy and impact, as if the roundel were a window
through which we look into a living scene. No one had thought
of this device before. Donatello was above all a realist: the bronze
panel which he did for Cosimo de' Medici of the martyrdom of St
Lawrence is so horrifying in describing the saint's death-agony
that this and its companion New Testament scenes may have
been too strong for the taste of the time and were not installed in
San Lorenzo until the sixteenth century. Equally horrifying, in its
own way, was the wooden statue of *St Mary Magdalen* in her
hideous old age, which may have been the sculptor's last work
(Museo dell' Opera del Duomo), and the great bronze of *St John
the Baptist*, still in its place in Siena Cathedral. Nothing like

these dramatic and tragic works had ever been produced before. Yet the bronze of *David*, which many would consider Donatello's finest work – it is certainly the best-loved – and which originally stood in the centre courtyard of the new Medici palace (it is now in the Bargello), is a work of fantastic imagination rather than realism. David is naked, and with his long hair and broad-brimmed hat is as beautiful as a girl, but is also a startlingly real youth; the audacity of the concept is shocking, exciting and suggestive, and one wonders what even the educated Florentine elite thought of it when it was first unveiled. But Donatello, then as always, did not care: he was serving his art and his God in the way that his genius – not society, or any other authority – dictated.

In the age of Donatello, highly gifted but still lesser artists tended to be overshadowed. But they were not overwhelmed, for by the early fifteenth century the art market in Italy was vast, and the cleverer ones looked carefully at his work to see what they could steal or, better, build upon into innovations of their own. Luca della Robbia (1399–1482), a younger Florentine contemporary, who got the commission for the great singing gallery in marble of the Florentine Cathedral organ-loft, was an artist who studied the antique as closely as Donatello, but who also liked to revive medieval imagery and effects when it suited him. His marble-carving is exquisite in its way, but he was quick to seize on Donatello's revival of terracotta as a material with huge commercial-artistic possibilities. In the 1430s he invented a tin-based glaze for terracotta, one of the great artistic discoveries of the period, indeed of all time. These powerful glazes both protect and intensify the colours, give the figures under them depth and luminosity, and bring out the beauty of the forms, making them significant and touching. The first work in this manner of which we have clear documentation dates from 1441, but glazed terra-cotta quickly became fashionable, partly because it was so immediately attractive, partly because it was comparatively cheap.

Luca della Robbia set up a highly productive workshop with his nephew, Andrea, and was soon exporting specimens over most of Europe. They could be taken to bits and reassembled, and so were easily transported, and they served not just as works of art in themselves, to decorate a *studiolo* or bedroom or dining-hall, but as elegant yet utilitarian objects in churches – tabernacles, holy-water stoups, reliquaries and stations of the cross. They could be used for grander purposes, such as major altarpieces, as well as roundels and ceiling bosses. Luca della Robbia was a delightful and charming artist rather than a great one, but his power to penetrate the European art market of his day was huge, and his influence therefore significant – he brought the Renaissance to many households below the princely level all over northern as well as southern Europe, and he had many imitators.

Nevertheless, in Italy at any rate the lead went increasingly to sculptors who aimed much higher, and especially to those who could produce the independent standing figure or, better still, the man on horseback. Halfway between the two sculptural giants, Donatello and Michelangelo, stands Andrea del Verrocchio (1435–88), yet another Florentine. His father was a brickmaker, perhaps a decorative one, and he was associated from an early age with the goldsmiths who, in Florence particularly, provided the skills and experimental environment from which so many great artists came. It is important to remember that most of the visually creative Renaissance leaders were artists in the widest sense: they could and often did turn their hands to architecture as well as painting and sculpture, to designs for almost any kind of artefact that required exceptional skill – to anything, in fact, for which there was or could be a market. If Verrocchio began as a goldsmith, he quickly turned to architecture as well, competing for major commissions, and became involved in a number of different metal projects, such as creating the giant copper ball for the lantern of Florence Cathedral. When he was senior enough to run a workshop of his own, which was also a retail shop where clients could come to buy, or order copies, or commission works of their choosing, he and his assistants worked in virtually all media and materials, from jewellery to massive bronzes and marbles, as well as monumental paintings and designs for architectural and display projects. His range and versatility – and enterprise – were reasons why so many talented young men, like Leonardo da Vinci, Perugino and Lorenzo di Credi, to list only the most celebrated, came to learn under his direction. Indeed, so successful was his shop that he opened another one in Venice.

Florentine artists, especially sculptors and painters, were highly competitive, and were encouraged to be so by their patrons, both municipal and private. Verrocchio was among the most competitive of all, both with other workshops, like that run by the Pollaiuolo brothers, and with individual artists, living or dead. His *Putto with a Dolphin* (Palazzo Vecchio, Florence) was an attempt to take over and surpass a favourite theme of antiquity, and a highly successful one. His *David* (Bargello) was a deliberate challenge to the youthful charm of the marvellous Donatello statue, and may well have been more popular in its day, for it is far more virile, and the detail is superb. His masterpiece, on which he spent much of the last decade of his life, was also an effort to surpass Donatello. Mounted figures, cast in bronze, life-size or larger, were regarded as one of the greatest achievements of antiquity. The four antique horses on St Mark's in Venice, stolen from Constantinople, were reminders of how difficult it was to sculpt and cast even unmounted equine statues. One of Donatello's greatest achievements, in the decade 1445–55, was successfully to create a mounted figure, the *Gattamelata*, in front of the great church of St Anthony in Padua. Verrocchio now outdid this, with his magnificent rendering of the mounted warlord Bartolommeo Colleoni, erected at one of the most prominent sites in Venice, just outside the church of SS Giovanni e Paolo. Technically it is a masterwork. Aesthetically, it is formidable, bringing out the terrifying brutality of the men who conducted warfare in the Renaissance. Indeed, it has some claims to be the most successful, as well as the best-known, of all mounted statues, and helps one to understand how Verrocchio contrived to extract such huge prices (up to 350 florins) out of his patrons.

One can probably learn more about Renaissance art from a detailed study of this industrious man's shops than from any other single institution. Behind the actual output were the preparatory drawings, the models or *bozzetti* in wax and clay, which were shown to clients to indicate what they could expect for their money, and the more finished *modelli* in terracotta. The shop and its back-studios and outhouses were full of equipment of every kind, including plaster models of actual heads, arms, hands, feet and knees, which Verrocchio had made by a secret process of his

THE ANATOMY OF RENAISSANCE SCULPTURE

own. These were used by himself and his assistants for sculpture and painting alike. He kept racks of drawings of male and female heads, and made clay models of figures, draped with rags dipped in plaster, for use in sculpting or painting drapery, a practice adopted by Leonardo and others who worked under him. Knowledge of the Verrocchio studio takes us behind the scenes of Renaissance art and shows how its high standards were based on intense discipline, careful preparation and a ruthless use of every mechanical aid that human ingenuity could devise. Behind this, in turn, was a passionate desire to make money as well as to produce the highest art.

It is important to note that Renaissance sculptors did not have to rely on plaster studio casts to emulate the antique. In a sense the antique was always around them, in the shape of arms and legs and heads of broken Roman statues, which were still to be found in Italy in large numbers at the close of the Middle Ages. From the fourteenth century they began to be prized by collectors and artists. Art-lovers would pay good prices for heads and torsos, and mount them in the courtyards of their city palaces or on the garden terraces of their country villas. Artists studied and copied them. Some were also employed by patrons to mend broken antiques and carve fresh bits to complete the figure, though this was work that well-known sculptors were too proud to undertake. But, just as scholars went in search of early manuscripts of classical works in monastery libraries, so artists rummaged through Roman ruins in search of artistic treasure. Whole statues in stone or marble were rare, and bronzes very scarce. The best in any case tended to be Roman copies of Greek originals. One bronze that did survive in a perfect state was the first-century AD *Spinario*, as it was called -- a nude boy taking a thorn from his foot. This rested on a column outside St John Lateran in Rome, near the bronze equestrian statue of Marcus Aurelius, and was much admired, especially by artists. It may well have inspired Donatello to create his *David*, just as the *Marcus Aurelius* undoubtedly encouraged him and Verrocchio to undertake equestrian bronzes. By the end of the fifteenth century, ambitious collectors were prepared to spend heavily on excavations of ancient sites likely to contain statuary. This was how the *Apollo Belvedere*, a genuine Greek statue, came to light in Rome in the 1490s, followed in 1506 by the *Laocoon*, one of the greatest masterpieces of antiquity. Both were acquired by Pope Julius II, who reigned 1503-13, and were the prize exhibits of his sculpture collections, which later formed the nucleus of the present Vatican Museum.

According to Vasari, studying the antique forms, not least in the palace of Julius II, was of critical importance to the work of the masters of what we call the High Renaissance, especially Leonardo, Raphael and Michelangelo. The last, in particular, learned from the ancients in all kinds of ways: design or *disegno*, choice of subject and materials, the actual carving, the finish, the balance between the parts and the whole, above all in developing a sense of monumentality, of grandeur, what the Italians call *terribilità*, the ability of art to inspire sheer awe. Michelangelo was born in Florence in 1475 and died in Rome eighty-eight years later. He had over seventy years of active artistic life, without pause or rest, working as sculptor, painter and architect, and writing poetry too. More nonsense has been written about him than about any other great artist: that he was a neurotic, a homosexual, a Neoplatonist mystic, etc. In fact he was nothing more than a very skilled and energetic artist, though often a very harassed one who got himself into contractual messes, not always of his own devising. He never thought about anything except getting on with his art as best he could, and worshipping God.

Michelangelo was primarily a sculptor, though it is probably true to say that he was more interested in the human form as such than in any particular way or medium for representing it. Obviously he found carving the best way of doing it, and his paintings tend to be two-dimensional sculptures. His wet-nurse was a stone-carver's wife from Settignano, and Michelangelo told Vasari that he 'sucked in the chisels and mallet' with her milk. His father was an ambitious, social-climbing bourgeois of Florence, who kept Michelangelo at school until he was thirteen and was most reluctant to allow him to sculpt for a living, believing it to be manual work and demeaning. This may explain why the boy was first apprenticed to a painter, Domenico Ghirlandaio, in 1488. Only in the following year did he manage to get himself into the sculpture garden workshop in the Medici house at San

Marco. He taught himself by copying the head of an antique faun, which attracted the attention of Lorenzo 'the Magnificent'.

Michelangelo was made when, at seventeen, he produced his first masterpiece, a marble relief, *The Battle of the Centaurs*. It is an exciting work, done with great facility and with striking economy, the nude male figures exhibiting extraordinary energy in punching the narrative home to the viewer. But it is unfinished, for reasons we do not know, and this became almost the hallmark of Michelangelo's work. However, he did finish his first important commission, a *Pietà* (Mary with the Dead Christ) intended for the tomb of a French cardinal in Rome and now in St Peter's. Michelangelo began it when he was twenty-two and completed the project to a high state of polish three years later. It is by any standards a mature and majestic work, combining strength (the Virgin) and pathos (the Christ), nobility and tenderness, a consciousness of human fragility and a countervailing human endurance, which fill those who study it with a powerful mixture of emotions. It is the ideal religious work, inducing reverence, gratitude, sorrow and prayer. The standard of carving, both of the flesh and the draperies, is without precedent in human history, and it is not hard to imagine the astonishment and respect it produced, among both cognoscenti and ordinary men and women. The youth of the sculptor made him a wonder, and the acclaim given to the work was the beginning of Michelangelo's reputation as an artistic superman, larger than life – like some of his works – and endowed with godly qualities.

Whether it benefits an artist to have this kind of reputation is debatable. Early in the sixteenth century, Michelangelo created from a gigantic marble block that had already been scratched at by earlier artists a heroic figure of *David*, designed to stand in the open (it is now in the Accademia, Florence) and overawe the Florentines. He omitted Goliath's head and the boy's sword, and the enormous work is a frightening statement of nude male power, carved with almost atrocious skill and energy. It made both Donatello's and Verrocchio's depictions seem insignificant by comparison and it added to the growing legend of Michelangelo's supranormal powers, patrons and public alike confusing the gigantism of the work with the man who made it. The year after he

67

finished it Julius II summoned him to Rome to create, for his own vanity and the admiration of posterity, a splendid marble tomb with a multiplicity of figures and a magnificent architectural setting. Michelangelo accepted with joy the chance to create such an ambitious work for a munificent patron, and he did indeed complete, to his satisfaction and everyone else's, at the time and since, part of the whole, a superb *Moses*, the godlike image of the lawgiver and judge who is the central figure in the Old Testament. Many would say it is the sculptor's finest work. But the entire project took forty years and was never finished as intended. It involved the artist in quarrels with the great, flights from Rome, lawsuits and endless anxiety, even a sense of failure. It destabilized Michelangelo as a man and an artist, drove him first into painting and then into large-scale architecture, and affected his attitude to work that had nothing to do with the tomb.

In the Accademia, Florence, there is the part-figure of the *Atlas Slave* for the tomb, really the torso and legs alone, the rest of the marble being cut to size but unworked. Why was it abandoned? We do not know. The *Dying Captive* (Louvre), also intended for the tomb, has the figure complete, and magnificent it is, but the supporting back and base are only roughly worked. Why? We do not know. Two marble tondos, of the Virgin and Child, one in the Bargello, Florence, the other the prize possession of the Royal Academy, London, are also incomplete, the superb faces and limbs emerging tentatively out of rough working. Time and again, Michelangelo conceived a grand or beautiful design, roughed it out, worked at it, completed part, and then left the rest, whether from lack of time, pressure of other commissions, dissatisfaction with his work or sheer exhaustion is rarely evident. Of course great artists sometimes prefer their work to be unfinished: it gives an impression of spontaneity and inspiration, which a meticulous veneer obscures. But in some cases, as in the great tomb of the Medici, with its awesome figure of the seated, pensive Lorenzo, itself complete as are the two supporting nudes beneath, niches are left empty and an air of incompleteness hovers over the whole.

Did Michelangelo suffer from some sickness of the soul? He was quarrelsome and often angry with himself as well as others. He seems to us an isolated figure, isolated in his greatness, in his lack of a private life or privacy, his heart empty of consummated love, his only competitor and measuring mark the Deity himself. It should also be said that Michelangelo imposed severe limitations on himself. He obviously did not like working in bronze, and rarely did so. It was an unlucky metal for him. His one great bronze effort, a gigantic statue of Julius II, was later melted down in an emergency and made into cannon. He made a wooden crucifix, and painted it. But in general he liked only marble, and carving with a high finish, and he preferred an elaborate architectural setting, so that his works are seen from the front, not in the round. All these self-imposed limits increased his difficulties, and Michelangelo was not an artist who, in times of stress, could console himself with creating small objects of beauty. Man and his work were on the grandest of scales, so that his triumphs were epic but so were his tragedies.

The superhuman great tend to blast and sterilize the territory around them. Michelangelo dwarfed his contemporaries in sculpture, and in the generation after his own no one took on his record. There was a time lapse of some decades before another heroic Italian, Bernini, put on Elijah's mantle, but by then the Renaissance was finally over and an entirely new epoch in European art, what we call the Baroque, had begun. The Italianized Fleming, Giambologna, who claimed to be an heir of Michelangelo, and who certainly attempted the heroic in marble and bronze, was also beyond the scope of the true Renaissance spirit. It is appropriate, however, to end this section with a reference to a contemporary of Michelangelo's middle and later years, Benvenuto Cellini (1500–71). He was in many ways the antithesis of Michelangelo as an artist, but he was a superbly characteristic Renaissance figure, in his love and knowledge of the antique, in his technical and artistic daring, in his amazing versatility, and in his love of human beauty, which was simultaneously complex and simple.

Like so many Renaissance practitioners of high art, Cellini came from that rich depository of skills, the Florentine artisanate. His grandfather was an expert mason and his father a specialized carpenter who among other things made and put up scaffolding for Leonardo da Vinci's large-scale projects, and carved advanced musical instruments. Cellini went into that Aladdin's cave and sorcerer's den of the Renaissance, a goldsmith's workshop. The skills he acquired there became the basis of an encyclopaedic knowledge of how to work with materials of all kinds, from gold and silver and the most precious of stones, to hard stones of every variety and base metals. Cellini was one of the few Renaissance artists trained as a goldsmith who is celebrated for a surviving piece of goldsmithing. Virtually all his early work vanished in the tragic sack of Rome in 1527, never to surface again, for, like bronze, gold was a risky material in which to seek eternal fame, as owners melted it down in hard times. However, Cellini worked for the munificent François I of France, 1540–5, and the superb gold and enamel salt he made for the king somehow came through to posterity and is now one of the greatest treasures of the Vienna Kunsthistorisches Museum. This enchanting object took Cellini two years to complete, which was regarded at the time as astonishing speed, and no wonder: no individual or team could produce it today in a century. If any one work of art, with its classical themes, its fecundity and brilliance, its adventurous technology and sheer love of art and humanity, sums up the entire Renaissance, it is this glorious extravaganza.

Cellini did so many different things that it is hard to list them all: ceremonial medals, with finely sculpted heads and ingenious reverses; coin dies, emblematic *enseignes*; the dies for seals – all of great artistry; elaborate candlesticks and ewers; altar furniture and tableware; small bronzes and decorative pieces of every description. He also aimed at the heroic and once or twice succeeded in achieving it, notably in his magnificent *Perseus and the Head of Medusa*, a large-scale bronze on an elaborate pedestal with a relief panel and four bronze statuettes in its niches. Commissioned by Cosimo de' Medici I and designed to stand in Florence's Piazza della Signoria alongside, and in competition with, Michelangelo's *David* and Donatello's *Judith and Holofernes*, it was finished in 1553 and seen by the sculptor as the climax of his career. The new Duke of Tuscany regarded it as the embodiment of his 'Etruscan revival' which his dukedom symbolized, for the pose recalls an Etruscan bronze of the fourth century BC, which Cosimo admired. This work, too, with its deliberate recall of the glorious antique past, and its brilliant display of what the artists of sixteenth-century Europe, and especially Florence, could now accomplish, was also a recapitulation, and epitome, of everything the Renaissance stood for.

The great bronze is perhaps the best-documented of any Renaissance work of art, for Cellini describes its conception and fabrication in considerable detail. He was a hot-blooded, rash, difficult and audacious man, with all the vices of artistic flamboyance that we associate with the more sensational Renaissance artists, and some peculiar to himself in addition. The surviving court records show him in and out of trouble all his life, often being forced to flee to escape trial. He was guilty of at least two killings, being pardoned by virtue of his artistic services – a typical Renaissance touch. He was twice accused of sodomy, the second time after the genesis of *Perseus*, causing him to flee to Venice, where he met the architect Sansovino, and Titian. He was nonetheless convicted, sentenced to four years in prison, and actually endured a long house arrest, which he used to write his autobiography. This delightful and highly informative work, a real window into the artistic world of his day, tells us all about the *Perseus* and many other works of his. It is also a work of literary art, which in its own way confirms the long process by which the humble and often anonymous medieval craftsman raised himself to the status of a Renaissance hero, albeit that in the violent and boastful Cellini's case he was more of an anti-hero. We learn from the autobiography that he was an art collector. Vasari says he amassed several cartoons from Michelangelo's Sistine Chapel ceiling, and he apparently copied out a treatise by Leonardo on the three arts of sculpture, painting and architecture, together with a study of perspective. The truth is, during the Renaissance, and especially in Florence, these arts were all closely interconnected, and from sculpture we now turn to the art of building.

PART FOUR

The Buildings of the Renaissance

To the ordinary citizens of late medieval Florence, or any other town in Italy, architecture was visually far more important than any other art, let alone writing. They might not penetrate to the treasures housed in the palaces, but they could see them from the outside, and they were familiar with the churches and the cathedrals, even being allowed into the sacristies, where the most precious art-objects were kept, on occasion. Building, even more than public sculpture, was a matter of civic pride. Italian citizens were also conscious of the architecture of antiquity, for its ruins were still there in many cases, not yet entirely looted for stone, tidied up or cleared away. In a sense, large parts of medieval Italy were still one vast architectural ruin, a constant reminder of the gigantism and glory of Rome, so that when increasing wealth encouraged the leading cities to glorify themselves in turn, it was to the example of their Roman past that artists naturally looked, and the public could compare the results. In architecture, then, the Renaissance was a natural event; it went with the grain of the country.

We have here a marked contrast between southern Europe, Italy in particular, and the North. Gothic had evolved in twelfth-century France out of Romanesque, itself a primitive, bastard form of the architecture of the late Roman Empire. But it had evolved into a style of its own, a truly original creation, eventually of great majesty and subtlety, embodying considerable engineering achievements, overwhelming decorative effects and impressive power. The major Gothic cathedrals of France, England, Germany and Spain are some of the largest and finest buildings ever constructed, and they became depositories of artistic treasures, only a fraction of which now remain. They were a wonder of the world, but they did not impress the Italians – even those who were aware of their existence or, a far smaller group, those who had seen them. Gothic was a habit, an impulse, not a system. It had no theory and no literature. It was a sophisticated evolution from a primitive instinct. Very few cathedrals were conceived and built as a whole, according to a master plan (Salisbury in England was a rare exception, and even in its case the spire was not added until 200 years later). Some, like Cologne, remained unfinished until modern times. The Italians, particularly in their northern plains, built Gothic cathedrals, such as Milan, but without enthusiasm or relish. The Gothic spirit, as opposed to forms, never settled upon them. There was something organic about it that Italians found unreasonable, so that one senses they adopted it only in an aberrant form and longed, perhaps unconsciously, to replace it with something better, derived from the roots of their culture.

In Florence, where the architecture of the Renaissance properly began, those roots were deep and they went back to Roman times. The cathedral was originally a building of the fifth or even the fourth century, which had twice been reconstructed in early medieval times. It was, then, a Roman-Romanesque work. The Baptistery, which is part of the complex, was modelled on the circular Pantheon in Rome, in the sixth or seventh centuries, though it was later altered and reconsecrated in 1059. So it too could be called a Roman work. The third building in the complex, the campanile or bell tower, was designed by Giotto di Bondone (1266–1337), more celebrated as a painter, who was made Master of the Cathedral Works in 1334. His plans survive, but he died three years later, and the actual building, constructed in turn by Andrea Pisano, the sculptor, and Francesco Talenti, is rather different. It does not look Gothic. But then it does not look Roman, or Romanesque, either. It is *sui generis*.

A generation before, in 1294, the Florentines decided they ought to pull down their old cathedral and build a new and bigger one, and a plan was drawn up two years later. The façade was built, of brick faced with white, green and pink marble, but work was suspended to build the campanile, in similar fashion, and the old cathedral was not finally demolished until 1375. By then the final design had been settled: a vast, oblong church with four immense bays between the façade and the sanctuary; an octagonal space surmounted by a great drum with a dome on top. The cathedral, as designed, was imagined in a splendid fresco, *The Church Triumphant*, painted by Andrea da Firenze, a member of the planning committee. But by whom and how was this monster, unprecedented in size and raising engineering problems that had never been tackled before, to be built?

The piers for the octagon were constructed 1384–1410; the drum was begun, and in 1418 a competition was held for the dome. It was won by Filippo Brunelleschi (1377–1446), in association with Ghiberti, who was of course already at work on the Baptistery doors. Brunelleschi guaranteed that the dome would not require construction by centring, the elaborate scaffolding process used in Gothic cathedrals to put up the stone vaults with which the masons covered large internal spaces. In fact a similar large internal space in Ely Cathedral in England, created earlier in the fourteenth century by the collapse of the central tower, had been filled by a gigantic piece of carpentry forming an octagonal lantern. But the Italians were not capable of high-level carpentry on this scale and may not have known about Ely anyway. They wanted a dome, and Brunelleschi turned to the Pantheon, the largest surviving dome from Roman times, for inspiration.

It should be understood that Brunelleschi was not, strictly speaking, the architect, since the size and form and indeed the actual curvature of the dome had been decided in 1367, ten years before he was born. He was rather the engineer, or as the contracts put it, 'the inventor and governor' of the project. He was an educated man, the son of a lawyer, intended for a learned profession until his brilliant drawing led him into goldsmithing, like most Florentine artists. He had been in competition with Ghiberti for the Baptistery doors, and after his rejection he went with Donatello to Rome to study the antique first-hand. He became a master of the details, as well as the forms, and the experience led him to make architecture his chief passion. He was, then, an intellectual. But he was also a scientist, in that he brought to the dome problem considerable knowledge of the practice of stress. The dome he designed, and carried to completion in 1436, rests on eight major ribs that continue the work of the piers beneath, assisted by sixteen minor ones, all being bound by horizontal strainer arches, and reinforced by metal tension-chains. The angle of the dome was made as steep as its form allowed, so that its construction was self-supporting, centrework being dispensed with. To make the weight carried lighter, Brunelleschi hit upon the device of an outer and inner skin, an invention of his own. Hence although the Pantheon dome was his inspiration, it was not his engineering model, since it had been built by the usual Roman frontal-assault methods of brute strength. Brunelleschi's dome was more sophisticated, more modern. The real test of his method, however, was not just the dome's stability but its external appearance, and it passed that triumphantly. The Florentines voted it a marvel, and indeed it still dominates the city in a way that few cathedrals do these days.

Brunelleschi emerged from the dome experience as a new kind of artist – the master-architect, as distinct from the craftsman or stonemason who had dominated medieval building. The architect was commissioned and paid by the patron, and he then directed and usually employed the craftsmen. Increasingly, too, the architect took charge of the design, rather than carried out a scheme laid down by a committee. Brunelleschi was a characteristic Renaissance figure, in that he carefully studied Roman and especially Etruscan models, and he certainly used elements from antiquity. But when we look carefully at what he produced, there is not much that is Roman about it, or Greek either. From 1419 he created the beautiful asylum for orphans, the Ospedale degli Innocenti, whose façade certainly employs the decorative vocabulary of classical architecture. But this spacious loggia of fragile Corinthian columns supporting semicircular arches, with roundels in the spandrels, surmounted by a deep entablature, is quite unlike anything the Romans ever built, in its slender grace and delicate proportion. It has sometimes been called the first true Renaissance building, and it introduced a design that could be adapted, and was, to countless different purposes over the coming centuries, and really has nothing to do with ancient Rome. It was a new style; indeed, a new way of beauty.

Brunelleschi used the same vocabulary, with his own additions, and amplified his original concepts, in his superb sacristy added to San Lorenzo in Florence, and in the Pazzi Chapel that he designed for another great Florentine church, Santa Croce. These airy, elegant, harmonious and wonderfully proportioned creations, with (in the case of the Pazzi Chapel) roundels by the ingenious della Robbia, and delicate colour schemes of grey and white, together with the natural colours of marble and brass, stone, iron and wood, delighted all who visited them, exuding as they did a princely simplicity in contrast to the Gothic clutter. To the artist who saw them for the first time, it was truly the shock of the new, not so much a revivification of antiquity as a realized beauty that he had never conceived and that made him itch to get out his pencil and work.

There are the unspoken elements of a theory behind Brunelleschi's creations: a simplification of parts, so that an orderly repetition becomes the norm, rather than an endless variety of inventions; a single system of lighting where possible; and a balance between the elements so that there is no dominant feature but a pervading style that brings the whole together. Moreover, in rejecting the Gothic and building upon the classical, he invented a new vocabulary of devices – curved entablatures as arches over columns, alternations of pillars and pilasters, scroll buttresses, alternations of flattened curves and flattened triangles, volutes and pendentives as punctuation marks – which made up a great part of the new vernacular that architects eagerly embraced, first in Italy, then everywhere. All this was presented by examples.

The theory was left to an intellectual of Florentine origins (though born in Genoa), Leon Battista Alberti (1404–72). Twenty-seven years Brunelleschi's junior, he got a university education in Bologna as well as a classical grounding at Padua. He was indeed much closer to the humanist writers than to the artist-craftsmen trained in goldsmithery, and was and remained a prolific writer all his life: comedies, philosophy, religion, ethics, various sciences, the care and riding of horses – these and many other matters he studied and put into print. As a secretary, first to a cardinal, then to Pope Eugenius IV in the 1430s, he learned the art of communication, and practised it. Eugenius took him to Rome, and there he engaged in archaeology, made a detailed study of Roman antiquities and was emboldened by what he saw to write a monumental series of aesthetic treatises, the first of any significance since Roman times, on sculpture, painting and, above all, architecture.

De Re Aedificatoria – Alberti usually wrote in Latin, which was later translated into Italian if there was a demand – was an elucidating, critical appraisal and reformulation of the great work of Vitruvius, *On Architecture*, the only work on the subject to come down to us from ancient times. (Alberti's treatise reached printed form in 1485, a year before Vitruvius' book was printed.) It is in every respect an improvement on Vitruvius', being clear, orderly, well written and good on theory and practice alike. He begins by giving the reader definitions, moves on to concepts, discusses materials, construction methods, town planning and the plans of different types of buildings. Then he goes on to consider the nature of beauty in architecture, and how it applies to religious, domestic and public buildings. He had an inquisitive and in some ways encyclopaedic mind, so a great many matters are dealt with, including water supply, archaeology, restoration and cost. It is the kind of book that every budding builder, and would-be architect, wanted to get his hands on, and could not until Alberti wrote it. And it has lasted: the way in which we approach architecture, distinguishing for instance between its basic, functional design, and its ornamental superfluities, is still Albertian.

Alberti also practised architecture, though not as a rule in the customary sense. He produced plans and designs that were executed with another architect in charge of the site. Thus the Palazzo Ruccelli in Florence was built on his instructions but with Bernardo Rossellini in charge (c. 1450) and the Malatesta church in Rimini, also by Alberti (c. 1447), was built by Matteo de' Pasti. He engaged directly in a number of important projects in and around the Vatican and Old St Peter's, but usually his plans and instructions for buildings, in places as diverse as Ferrara and Mantua, were sent by messenger. In some cases Alberti never even saw the creations for which he was ultimately responsible. His influence was nonetheless wide and pervasive, perhaps even more so than Brunelleschi's. Not that Alberti ever underrated the older master. On the contrary, his admiration overflowed. His first sight of the great Florence dome was the central aesthetic experience of his life, and he wrote: 'Who could ever be so cold or envious as to fail to recognize the genius of an architect capable of creating such an enormous structure, rising into the sky, big enough to cover all the people of Tuscany with its shadow – and all done without the aid of centring or even much scaffolding?' Alberti cited the dome as an example of how modern Florentine artists – and others – could not merely imitate the ancients but surpass them. That, he maintained, was the object: to build on the past even finer and more audacious structures. However, the study of the past came first. Alberti saw Brunelleschi's work as in some respects only a superficial departure from medieval barbarism – his ground plans still tended to be non-classical.

Alberti altered all that, and his designs were classical in inspiration from start to finish, and from top to bottom. After his instructions were followed, and his plans, as well as his book, circulated throughout Italy, it became rare for any architect, creating a church, *ab initio*, to use a simple east-west axis. The old west front became a classical façade, created round a door that led into a space, usually circular or octagonal; the east end choir disappeared, and all the activities of the edifice revolved round a central point. However, Alberti was not a man who preached rigid uniformity. He also used the Greek cross as a floor plan, and he sometimes combined a circular rotunda with a short nave. His façades divided into three main prototypes. He rang the changes with the different classical orders and he formulated alternative schemes of fenestration. But in doing all this he was merely, as it were, completing the architectural vernacular of the new style. Brunelleschi introduced it; Alberti turned it into a complete system, which students could absorb until it became second nature to them. Thus Alberti set patterns in the visual appearance of buildings, especially their main façades, which were replicated in essentials for centuries, and are still with us.

We must not think, however, that the newly emerging architectural face of Italy was entirely the work of one or two men of genius. In fact there were hundreds of journeyman architects, and one or two massive wheel-horses whose contributions were truly monumental. The outstanding example of this group was Michelozzo (Michelozzi) di Bartolommeo (1396–1472). He eventually became personal architect to Cosimo de' Medici and a favourite among rich patrons because he was willing to tailor his designs to suit their views (he was in fact the son of a Florentine tailor). He had all-round talent and experience, working first in the mint, on coin design, then in Ghiberti's shop, then in a collaborative sculptural practice with Donatello. Indeed, he designed and made bronze fittings, marble and precious metal tabernacles and other church furniture, and elaborate tombs, all his life. When Brunelleschi died, he became Master of the Cathedral Works – in effect head of the architectural profession in Florence – and set up the magnificent lantern that Brunelleschi had designed to cap his dome.

Michelozzo had no architectural theories. He loved the antique. He had no objections to medieval styles. A lot of his work was patching up or extending or rebuilding existing edifices, so that he had to respect the past whatever it was. He merged Gothic elements with the new Renaissance patterns. The monastery he built at Bosco ai Frati is essentially medieval. His façade for the town hall at Montepulciano is almost a replica of the Palazzo Vecchio in Florence. He remodelled the Medicis' beautiful villa at Trebbio with Renaissance touches but it still looks like a castellated medieval fortress. There are medieval touches and irregularities in another villa he built at Cafaggiolo, though it is notable that building and garden are delightfully integrated in a way that would not have been possible in a fortified, moated medieval country residence, but which was to be characteristic of Italy from about 1440 on (and soon of all civilized Europe).

But Michelozzo was also an innovator. In the monastery of San Marco, Florence, he built the first Renaissance library – a long, elegant room entirely designed to house and display books. Here again he took the idea of the layout, with its aisles and recesses, from a medieval source, a typical fourteenth-century monastic dormitory, but with books resting where monks once slept. He built a chapel for the Medici at Santa Croce that is simple, neat, elegant and in the Renaissance vernacular, so that many other architects copied it, but it still had a bit of medieval-style vaulting. The town palace he built for the Medici in Florence, with its central courtyard on classical arches, its huge external cornices frowning onto the street, and its delightful garden and loggia, became one of the most popular buildings of the entire Renaissance, to judge by the number of times it was copied or looted for ideas. It was supplemented by another Medici country house, which is the first attempt to revive the Roman villa, with no pretence at fortification, and the garden is as integral to the design as the walls. This too was replicated again and again. Michelozzo was also daring in taking ideas from the Temple of Minerva in Rome and using them for the tribune of the Annunziata in Florence, built as a circle with nine chapels leading off it.

In short, he combined old and new, as a good architect should, to please his clients. But he had no genius, as such, and his amiability and desire to please changed to irritability and moodiness as his busy career progressed. That is the life pattern of many architects, who have the difficult job of standing between exigent and changeable clients, and tardy and often incompetent workmen, while the costs soar and bills are unpaid. He was very skilled at dealing with water, so that anything to do with moating, hydraulics and damp-coursing was his delight. He had to fall back on this after 1460, when he lost his key job in Florence and ended up in remote Ragusa, supervising its sea-girt city walls – a sad declension. But most of the architects of the Renaissance saw a tailing off in their popularity as they aged and new men with fresh ideas prised their fingers from the raft of success.

An exception was Donato Bramante (1443–1514), whose most important and innovative work was done towards the end of his life. He came from Urbino, which was part of the papal states, and his achievement reflects the way in which, in the last quarter of the fifteenth century, the architectural centre of Italy was shifting from Florence to Rome. As soon as he could read and write he was put to painting and perspective, and may have been taught by Mantegna. He was close to the high-powered artistic court of the great Federigo da Montefeltro, where Alberti was a visitor, and he witnessed the construction of the duke's tremendous palace by Luciano Laurana, where Piera della Francesca was also at work. He came to architecture via a fascination for perspective drawings, one of which survives as an engraving. By the time he started work designing buildings, first for the Sforza dukes of Milan, and elsewhere in Lombardy, he was already developing a taste for the monumentally gigantic, which was quite new, and was closer to the hugeness of ancient Rome than the elegant creations of the Florentines, with their stress on slender columns and graceful arches.

Bramante's first important work, the miracle-church of Santa Maria presso San Satiro, Milan, though small in itself, has a novel grandeur based on massive piers and pilasters. In 1492, he did a new east end or tribune for the church of Santa Maria delle Grazie in Milan, a monumental concoction of apsidal recesses based on huge square piers, which carries his ideas of an awe-inspiring structure enclosing vast spaces much further. He got further practice in the monumental by helping in the rebuilding of Pavia Cathedral, which was recast as a Greek cross forming the centre of a vast octagon – obviously Bramante's idea, though others were involved. The Milan duke also gave Bramante the opportunity to design a stunning courtyard, with ingenious use of a variety of Roman-style columns and pilasters, for the Abbey of Sant' Ambroglio, and perhaps more important the layout of a new square in the nearby town of Vigevano. This involved the demolition of an old quarter and its replacement by an open Renaissance space of vast size as a setting for the cathedral – a critical step forward in a process that was soon to cover the capitals of Europe with monumental squares and oblongs.

By this point in his career it was evident that Bramante's work was dominated not so much by the erection of buildings in itself as the function they served – to enclose huge areas of internal space in a way that staggered the beholder. By a fortunate coincidence, the collapse of Sforza rule in Milan in 1499 drove Bramante to Rome, where there were better opportunities for him to express his grandiose ideas, first under the Borgia pope, Alexander VI, then under the great Julius II (pope 1503–13). Julius was obsessed by power, which he expressed both in building up the papal states as a major force, militarily and financially, and in reviving the glories of Rome, as an imperial city, by an enormous programme of building. Even before Julius received the tiara, Bramante made his mark by creating impressive courtyards and palaces, and by producing carefully measured studies of major buildings from antiquity, not only in Rome but at Tivoli, Caserta and Naples. The fruits of his efforts to understand and express the antique were seen in what is now called the Tempietto, the one building of the entire Renaissance that comes close to perfection. This is a circular stone chapel, with columns and dome, covering the exact spot where, it was thought, St Peter was martyred in Rome. It is a combination of features based upon a number of Roman prototype-temples. It follows strictly the Vitruvian rules of proportion, the measurements of the elevations and units being multiples of the diameter of the columns, which is the modal norm. It uses the Doric order and is the first Renaissance building to be decorated with metopes and triglyphs in a regular Doric frieze. But it is at the same time an entirely original building, for the outer columns are echoed by the pilasters supporting the inner drum, something the Romans would never have done, and the building as a whole is not Roman in appearance at all – it is unmistakably Renaissance. It has the further quality that, though small, it exhibits all the dignity of a building of vast dimensions: in short, it is the architect's dream of monumentality achieved by minimal means.

With Julius II on the papal throne, Bramante was soon able to realize his soaring ambitions in earnest. He began work on the prodigious extension of the Vatican Palace known as the Cortile del Belvedere. This has grand terraces and breathtaking internal and external vistas, some of them designed to delight the ambitious eye of the pope as he peered at them from his bedroom window as soon as he woke in the morning. Part of the complex incorporates an ingenious and grand spiral staircase or ramp, which takes the visitor from top to bottom of the building, through its various floors. Near the base, the columns are Tuscan; then they become Doric and, in ascending order, Ionic and Composite, and these gradations are repeated in the various floors of the palace. Thus Bramante had hit on a new way of emphasizing the variety of the decorative forms of antiquity by allowing each to dominate a particular floor. He used the same device in the façade he designed for the superb Palazzo Caprini (1510), where the ground or street floor is heavily rusticated in massive stone blocks, with curved archway-windows, as though for a fortress, and the *piano nobile* above it is held up with slender Doric twin columns framing elegant palatial windows. This delightful trick of having two building designs in one, another instance of grandeur and profusion achieved by modest means, was later imitated in thousands of formal buildings all over Italy and Europe – indeed, it became one of the most common architectural clichés of all time. It was a sign of the times, and of the increased fame, prominence and wealth of individual artists in the Italy of the High Renaissance, that this wonderful creation was bought by Raphael in 1517 as his town house.

Bramante worked on many churches in Rome, notably Santa Maria del Popolo, and elsewhere in the neighbourhood, like the church of SS Celso e Giuliano, but his principal efforts were concentrated on Julius II's plans for a new St Peter's. His ideas and Bramante's coincided: that it was time to wipe the slate clean and replace the old basilica, which both thought barbarous, with one embodying the principles of the new antique-based architecture; that this project should be completed on the largest possible scale, to show that the new Rome now arising was superior to its imperial, pagan past; and that the building should exhibit the space-enclosure now made possible by engineering experience, and which was most calculated to impress vast congregations during the pontifical services. For inspiration, Bramante looked to what had been the largest roofed buildings in ancient Rome, the enormous public baths, especially those of Caracalla, whose piers and circular openings supported roofs enclosing spaces that even Renaissance man found unimaginable.

Actually, the ambitious Bramante had no need of inspiration from antiquity, since most of his ideas for the new St Peter's had already been adumbrated by his work in Lombardy, notably in Santa Maria delle Grazie and Pavia Cathedral. The chief difference was the increased size. Size may not be the most important element in architecture as a rule, but it is in buildings aiming to awe. Many people worked innumerable modifications to his original plan. But it was he who gave the church its salient element, both inside and out – sheer size. Whether seen from ten miles away, eructing in the Rome skyline, or glimpsed from across the city, or nearer to from the space between the enclosing arms of its vast colonnade, or goggled at from within, St Peter's is the crowned monarch of ecclesiastical architecture. There is nothing like it anywhere, and scale is the key to its uniqueness.

Having said this, however, it must be admitted that the architectural history of the new St Peter's is extremely complicated. A truly great church appears to have a vigorous life of its own, and at times the architects successively connected with it seem little more than flies buzzing round the site. Work on the proposed site for the new church had actually begun as far back as 1452, under Bernardo Rossellino, and the foundations then laid had a permanent effect on the structures later placed upon them, like a palimpsest emerging through the writing that covers it. There were various stops and starts before Bramante took over. His first plan on paper (1506), a beautiful affair in orange wash and brown ink, actually survives. It envisaged a centralized, square church, with four subsidiary domes as well as the main one. One of his assistants, Giuliano da Sangallo, criticized this concept, and Bramante scrapped it for a more longitudinal shape. When Julius II died, there were further changes, under the new pope Leo X, a Medici with ideas of his own. The central piers, though reduced in size, had been completed when Bramante himself died in 1514. Sangallo and his other assistant, Fra Giocondo, then took over, but the pope put the young Raphael of Urbino (1483–1520) in overall charge. Raphael abandoned some of Bramante's ideas but in other ways he reverted to his original plan, adding bits of his own. But he too died in 1520, and his amendments were either never built or demolished. Sangallo produced an alternative which survives as a wooden model. But the sack of Rome, and subsequent lack of cash, prevented much from being done. Sangallo in turn died in 1546, whereupon the ageing Michelangelo (he was seventy) was told to take over. He produced yet another plan, which involved clearing out the Raphael–Sangallo completed portions more or less entirely, and again reverting to Bramante. So much of the present interior is essentially Michelangelo's work, but following Bramante's idea.

Michelangelo was obsessed by the dome, and produced a number of designs leaning heavily on Brunelleschi's Florentine dome. What he eventually produced is much more complicated and monumental, with strongly articulated curved buttresses descending into twin columns outside the drum. He actually built the drum, but when he died in 1564, no work had been done on the dome. By now the pope was Pius IV, who told the two new architects, Pirro Ligorio and Giacomo Vignola, to carry out Michelangelo's plans without argument. Pirro ignored this injunction, started his own work on the attic inside the dome, and was sacked. Vignola reintroduced the idea of subsidiary domes, which Bramante had abandoned over sixty years before, and his successor, Giacomo della Porta, actually built two flanking domes, as we see them today. He demolished what was left of Bramante's choir, vaulted Michelangelo's dome, but increased the rake, and this meant that the outer shell is much steeper than Michelangelo's broad shape, as well as nearly thirty feet higher. The dome was complete by 1593, but della Porta had to employ an engineer, Domenico Fontana, to work out the stresses, something none of his predecessors would have done, and evidence of the increasing specialization of the building industry, now operating with colossal masses. However, in architecture what matters is what is actually put up, and remains put up. Della Porta's dome is markedly different in silhouette from Michelangelo's, but it was built, and after a few years began to look not only right but inevitable. So his is the great dome-shape that was imitated throughout Rome and eventually all over Europe. Thus della Porta, not a great architect, certainly became an influential one.

There remained the façade, which had also been designed by Michelangelo, on a scale and width that even Bramante might have thought a touch too grandiose. It was more like an emperor's palace than the front of a church, with its giant pilasters and pillars and endless bays. The spirit of this design was eventually carried out, by a succession of five architects, culminating in the great Gianlorenzo Bernini (1598–1680), who completed the work and then went on to lay out the piazza in front of the church, with its flanking colonnades, finished in 1667. Thus this great church took over two centuries to be built, and was the work of more than a dozen architects under thirty-two popes, some of whom interfered directly and imposed their own ideas or vetoes, and it spanned the mid-fifteenth-century Renaissance, the High Renaissance and the Baroque. (I am ignoring the sacristy and the clocks, the work of Rococo times.) This wonderful building, closely examined, bears all the marks of its long evolution and manifold progenitors. Yet, as with its dome, because we are used to it, it looks right, as though the endless squabbles, changes of plan and demolitions had never been. It illustrates the problem of writing architectural history, and indeed of being an architect, who can never be in quite the same control of his work as a painter or sculptor is. So: who built St Peter's? The answer is, God and time built St Peter's, but insofar as any one man did it, it was Bramante.

Michelangelo's proposed façade for St Peter's, which embroiders on rather than reflects the interior it conceals, and is wider too, breaks all the rules of architecture, as laid down by Vitruvius, Alberti or anyone else. And the reason for this is that Michelangelo did not enter the art or trade as a novice, eager to learn, but as a world-famous sculptor, more anxious to teach. His grandiose sculptural schemes required appropriate architectural settings. The settings required appropriate churches, or other buildings, to house them. The search for appropriateness, therefore, produced a natural progression from sculpting to architecture. The first work for which he was responsible was in the great pontifical fortresses of Sant' Angelo in Rome (1515–16). It is punctuated with sculptural devices as though the itch to carve was still stronger than the need to tell workmen what to do. Leo, a Medici, also wanted Michelangelo to complete the family church of San Lorenzo in Florence with a marble sculptured façade, and drawings and a wooden model for this project survive. But there were disagreements and quarrels over the cost of the proposal and nothing came of it.

Michelangelo did, however, carry out two works for another Medici pope, Clement VII, at San Lorenzo – a sacristy and a library. Both are based on ideas he plucked from antiquity, both ignore Vitruvian and any other rules, and both exhibit the fertility of his imagination. He made up his architectural vernacular as he went along, improvising and inventing, so that nothing he did is like anything done before by others, or even by himself. His contemporaries and successors found this disconcerting and Vasari criticized him as a rule-breaker. The sacristy is really a tomb-depository for Medici grandees, which suited Michelangelo, a tomb-designer turned architect, and his details are extraordinarily inventive. But they overwhelm the whole, which lacks unity. It should be regarded as a preparation for the Laurentian Library and its vestibule, which came later (1524, completed 1562).

For this library, and its staggering stair-approach, Michelangelo turned architecture outside in, that is he used the structural features one finds on the outside of a building as decorative features for the interior. Windows, whether oblong or square, become blind recesses or tabernacles; entrances become doors or mere punctuations in blank walls; pillars or pilasters, instead of supporting the roof, frame the non-windows; while the ceiling reflects the decorative non-functionalism of the walls rather than suggests how it hangs there or what architectural machinery it conceals. There are all kinds of ingenious inventions that catch and delight the eye, and the style of everything is consciously classical, or rather classicism as reinvented by Michelangelo. Yet one cannot help feeling that he was unconsciously following the same exuberant route of the late Gothic stonemason-architects, who turned functional forms into wildly extravagant ornaments.

This progress from use into fancy is carried still further in the vestibule staircase, from which the visitor ascends from the church cloister into the library. The elegant sets of windows let in no light and serve no function save decoration, the beautiful marble columns support nothing, and the three-pronged staircase achieves no purpose by its complexities save to delight the eye. Michelangelo defended it by saying that the servants would line the outer steps on each side while their masters processed up or down the central stairs. But this is an excuse, not a reason. On the other hand, the whole thing is enchanting, in colour no less than in form, and the details, as always with this master, are beautifully inventive. The marble is served up crisply, as befits an accomplished chisel-man, and there is an inherent simplicity about it all that allows you to take in the concept as a whole and then turn to its highly imaginative parts. No work more clearly demonstrates what distinguishes great architecture from the routine. But Michelangelo's manner is prominent in every inch:

it is mannered, and it set mankind on the long trek from the High
Renaissance, through Mannerism to the Baroque and so to Rococo.
This staircase hall is the distant ancestor, by direct descent, of
the vast Treppelhaus in the Bishop's Palace at Würzburg, which
Tiepolo turned into the largest artistic artefact in world history.

From this wonderful concept in Florence, Michelangelo
returned to Rome to design and (largely) complete a great outdoor
architectural scheme, the Piazza del Campidoglio on the Capitoline Hill. This began when Paul III moved the famous antique
equestrian statue of Marcus Aurelius, which had inspired Donatello's and Verrocchio's efforts in the genre, from the Lateran Palace,
and asked Michelangelo to design a new base. The great sculptor,
in characteristic fashion, began by creating an elegant but imposing overall base for the huge work, then opened up the project into
an enormous architectural setting, with a decorative pavement, a
monumental staircase-ramp, a new façade for the building at the
top of it, the Palazzo Senatorio, and new flanking buildings on
either side. The whole splendid composition may have evolved
organically as the master proceeded, or it may have been in his
mind from the start, or a bit of both. It finally involved further
oval steps below the pavement, and the resulting ensemble has a
naturalness and simplicity and yet an impressive grandeur that
belies its accidental origins. No one of any sensibility can fail to
delight in walking about it, taking it in as a whole, and relishing
its felicitous details.

Michelangelo's heavy and often frustrating work on St Peter's
dominated the last part of his life, but he engaged in other projects,
which included work on the Farnese Palace and Santa Maria degli
Angeli in Rome. He also designed a monumental city gate in
Rome, the Porta Pia, which ended a new street of magnificent
houses and gardens pushed out from the Quirinale by Pope Pius
IV. All these works, and others, some of which survive only in
designs and plans, complete the vernacular of Michelangelo's
architecture, a rich vocabulary of lion's heads, egg-and-darts,
dentils and acanthus leaves, coats of arms and crenellations pulled
from the Middle Ages, grinning masks and triglyphs, and all the
orders of antiquity, plus composites of his own invention, broken
pediments, sphinxes supporting closed ones, swags, receding and

overlapping planes, echoes of Doric, Corinthian and Ionic capitals flaunted as decorative features, and his characteristic inversions – façades introduced as profiles and vice versa. The fertility is awe-inspiring and at times overwhelming; also pathetic and moving, considering that some of these explosions of the imagination occurred when the old man was in his eighties, an immense age for those days. They swirled away into history to become the stock-in-trade of professional mediocrities for hundreds of years, and the base on which the few geniuses of the seventeenth and eighteenth centuries wrought marvels. It is likely that Michelangelo found his architectural career as frustrating as his sculptural one, but the consequences of both, often overlapping, resonate through the ages.

Many of these wonderful decorative devices were eventually to find natural homes in Venice, where Michelangelo's exuberance was the norm, though he never, alas, worked there. Venice came only slowly to the Renaissance, perhaps because it was by history and instinct a profoundly Gothic city (and, if Ruskin could have had his way, would have remained exclusively so). Indeed, it is Italy's only genuine Gothic city. But, by a curious paradox, the fall of Constantinople in 1453, which should have extinguished its prosperity, actually increased it, initially at least, and led Venice to expand inward, thus linking it more firmly to Renaissance developments at a time when it was anxious to spend money on its visual aggrandizement. Renaissance architecture was brought to the city in the 1470s from outside, chiefly by Pietro Lombardo and Mauro Codussi, who were responsible for the Scuola Grande at St Mark's, Santa Maria dei Miracoli (Lombardo), San Michele in Isola (Codussi) and Santa Maria Formosa (Codussi), as well as many palaces, such as the Palazzo Corner-Spinelli and the Palazzo Loredan.

In 1527 the brilliant Florentine artist Jacopo Sansovino (1486–1570) settled in Venice. He had begun life as a sculptor, but had formed contracts with the ramifying Sangallo family who provided no less than five prominent Renaissance architects. Sansovino reconstructed the entire San Marco area, providing the mint or Zecca, the logetta at the bottom of the campanile, completing the piazza, clearing the Piazzetta and building opposite the Doge's

Palace the beautiful St Mark's Library (Libreria Marciana). He also built one of the grandest Renaissance palaces, the Palazzo Dolfin (1538), which shows the influence of the treatise published the year before by Sebastiano Serlia, Venice's contribution to architectural theory. By this point, architects were thriving in the city. They included Antonio Scarpagnino, who built the Scuola Grande di San Rocco, the Fondaco dei Tedeschi, the Fabbriche Vecchie and the Palazzo dei Dieci Savi, and Michele Sanmicheli, responsible for the magnificent Palazzo Grimani as well as the Palazzo Corner at San Polo. The contract to design the new Rialto Bridge was won by Antonio da Ponte (1588), in competition not only with Sansovino but with a proposal made earlier by Andrea Palladio (1508–80).

Palladio ranks as Venice's greatest architect, indeed, one of the greatest in Italian history. But he actually came from Padua, where he was trained as a stonemason. At the age of sixteen he broke his contract and went to Vicenza, where he worked on decorative sculptures and formed contacts with the local rich – he was, says his first biographer, Paolo Gualdo, 'an extremely social man'. He did villa-work for the poet Giangiorgio Trissino, who gave him the name 'Palladio', the angelic messenger in the epic he was writing; and he also met the Paduan theorist Alvise Cornaro, whose palace had an odeon and a loggia designed by Giovanni Maria Falconetto, among the earliest Renaissance buildings in the area (1524–30). Trissino took him to Rome (1541) to study antiquities and see what was being built there, and he returned to the city on similar expeditions on four more occasions. Though not formally educated, then, Palladio was the scholar type of architect, who knew all the treatises available and helped to translate Vitruvius, providing beautiful illustrations. Indeed, his drawings are central to his work.

Palladio believed in drama; he believed in settings. He placed his buildings in their surroundings in his mind's eye, before he set to work designing them, so that they all have a geographical and spatial context. He was an architect who not only drew but who painted his buildings into the scene. The mind boggles at what he might have accomplished in Rome, where all the buildings are part of a gigantic and historic urban landscape. As it was,

Venice provided an equally exciting setting for his imagination, and his work on the island of San Giorgio Maggiore, across the basin from St Mark's, altered the visual skyline of Venice permanently and gave the city much of the magic we all love. He built the refectory of the San Giorgio monastery there, making it both simple, even severe, and monumental (1560). The monks were so pleased they commissioned him to rebuild their church. The result was magnificent, seen from across the water from the Piazzetta – dramatic, elegant, almost ethereal, depending on the season and the weather. That of course was how it was meant to be seen. Looked at close to, it is less impressive, and the interior disappoints, Palladio not being a man who thought primarily of churches as places of worship. It was, then, a vision, not based on any classical model or recent creation by Brunelleschi, Alberti *et al.*, but *sui generis*, a piece of wonderful stage-scenery. It has been criticized, but no one who has seen it – Ruskin apart – would wish it changed.

His other great Venetian church, the Redentore, is more carefully designed for use, though its peculiarity as a votive church, where the rich made solemn vows and gave thanks for mercies, often in the form of huge processions, demanded theatrical effects. The water-façade, from which it is entered, is a virtuoso display of the classical orders and proportions, crowned by giant statues, and is another of the great sights of Venice, with the dome and spires crouching behind and constantly changing their relationship to the front as you come up to it by gondola. The interior of the church, however, also functions well and has always been much used.

In fact, while Palladio had a taste and a genius for theatrical effects, and could be quite ruthless at achieving them at the expense of function, he was fundamentally, odd as it may seem, a practical architect who designed his buildings for use. Most of his life he spent designing villas or country houses, and he set out his principles. In 1570 he published his *Quattro libri dell'architettura*, four books that describe, in order: general principles and technology; private residential buildings; public secular buildings; and antique temples. In the second of these he insists that the villa is the centre of an agricultural estate. It must be situated, therefore, with a view to the well-being of the land, so that the owner may supervise it properly. And it must be built with agricultural aspects in mind – however noble and imposing, the farm must be catered for in the structure.

Moreover, although Palladio was a classical architect, in that he knew and understood everything about the theory and practice of antiquity – insofar as the knowledge was then available – he insisted that he followed the antique because it was functional as well as beautiful. He did not hesitate to introduce his own fundamental modifications of design when they added to utility, though he ensured they added grace too. This firm foundation of sense, and flexibility of execution, help to explain why he was so successful in his day, why his houses work as well as please, and why they were so generally followed for generations, all over Europe.

Palladio never repeated himself. Each design is a little world in itself. The Villa Godi-Malinverni, the Palazzo Chiericati and the Palazzo della Ragione, all in or near Vicenza, the Villa Cornaro, near Treviso, and the Villa Rotonda, at Vicenza, are all very different; and the Villa Serego, near Verona, with its all-rusticated surface, surprises people when they are told Palladio was the architect, as it seems so uncharacteristic. But all these works, and others, on close inspection, are seen to embody Palladio's principles: attention to climate and setting; serving to impress from afar and offer service and comfort within; radiating order and economy as well as utility; and making the most intelligent possible use of sun and shade, varying materials, angles, different façades and surrounding gardens and plantations. His most famous villa, the Rotonda, with its imposing Ionic façades on each side of a domed square, looks like a house to impress rather than to live in. Not so. It works very well. The combination of beauty and functionalism, of grandeur and utility, explains why Palladio was so much in demand by rich men (and their wives) who loved display but took a practical approach to estate management and farming; had to, indeed, to be able to afford what the master provided for them.

His practice flourished, and in due course these buildings, and what he wrote about them, became known all over Europe, and were imitated and adapted to different climates and latitudes. Thus the Palladian style was born, spread, in time crossed the Atlantic, and went east to India and beyond. He was the only one of the Renaissance architects to give his name to a style, which has endured. He was also the last of the true Renaissance architects – that is, men inspired by a love and knowledge of the antique, especially Roman, past, who wanted to recreate its best features, suitably modified, in the sunny cities and countryside of fifteenth- and sixteenth-century Italy. By the time he died, in 1580, the work of the Renaissance, in Italy at least, was complete, and its buildings were spread out for men to see, to love, to learn from and to be warned by; and a different spirit was in the air.

PART FIVE

The Apostolic Successions of Renaissance Painting

The history of painting during the Renaissance is enormously complicated and involves hundreds of good or outstanding painters, operating over a huge geographical area for the best part of 300 years. In order to understand it, certain salient points must be grasped from the beginning. And the first point concerns visualization – that is, the way in which painters analysed the visual world with their eyes and brains, and transferred what they saw to a two-dimensional surface. In deep antiquity, particularly in Egypt, the early civilization where the arts were most strongly developed, the visualization was aspective: that is, the artist, working in paint or low-relief sculpture, conveyed to his two-dimensional surface not so much what he saw, as what he knew was there. All the details that he felt were significant for his purpose, not just those to be seen from a single viewpoint, were systematically put down. The result is real and truthful in the sense that everything represented *is* there, and so the information conveyed is exact. But the eye does not see it, or all of it, so in another sense it looks false or clumsy or primitive.

Since the artist is striving to create illusion, to produce a two-dimensional something that looks exactly like the real thing, he is never content with aspective art, unless (as in ancient Egypt) he is constrained by canonical conventions laid down by religious dogma. The ancient Greeks were subject to no such constraints, or freed themselves from them; so that from the seventh century BC, and especially during the classic period of Greek art in the fifth century BC, they developed various devices, such as foreshortening of the human figure, and the use of perspective, to create two-dimensional illusions of reality. This replacement of aspective art by perspective art is one of the greatest steps forward in human civilization. It is not always easy to follow, since virtually no Greek wall-painting survives. What does survive is usually on the curved or spheroid surfaces of painted vases and other utensils. The Greeks learned not only to portray the human body as it is seen, but to present it in realistic action, and in the context of its surroundings. By foreshortening and other illusionistic devices, and by deploying perspective conjunctions, they contrived to conquer pictorial space, just as in the twentieth century we began to conquer astronomic space. The Romans inherited their knowledge and skills, and some of their flat-surface painting does survive, notably at Pompeii. In the Wall of the Corinthian Oecus, in a wall from the villa of Publius Fannius Sinistor, and in friezes from the house of Marcus Lucretius Fronto, we see three examples of the effective use of linear and aerial perspective, foreshortenings and other tricks.

In late antiquity, or early in what we call the Dark Ages, this form of sophisticated illusionary art disappeared, and its techniques were lost. The loss applied as much to the Greek world of Byzantium, where the empire of Rome survived in debased and truncated form, as in the Latin West, where it disappeared completely. Artists reverted to the primitive visual technology of aspective art, both on two-dimensional surfaces, such as wall-painting and illuminated manuscripts, and in low-relief and sculpture. However, enough survived of illusionism, in the Byzantine world and in Italy, for artists to note it and in due course to imitate it. From the twelfth and thirteenth centuries, there was a classicizing revival in the Byzantine Empire, most notably expressed in wall-paintings in the church of St Nicholas, at Boyana in what is now Bulgaria, which are dated 1259. Similar, and possibly quite unconnected developments took place in central Italy, at a somewhat later date. First Cimabue (1240–1302), then Duccio di Buoninsegna (1260–1320) and Giotto di Bondone (1267–1337), in Siena, Florence and elsewhere, began to use foreshortening and various forms of perspective. These key developments can be seen in various churches, especially Cimabue's wall-paintings in the Upper Church of San Francesco in Assisi, and Giotto's work in the Arena Chapel in Padua, and in the Bardi and Peruzzi Chapels at Santa Croce in Florence.

These changes were pushed further by artists such as Masaccio (1401–28) and by the sculptors Ghiberti and Donatello. Early users of linear perspective, such as Giotto, tended to employ it instinctively, without ocular aids, as many artists have done ever since. But there are hints in Vitruvius that the Romans, and possibly the Greeks before them, had a 'scientific' method. Early in the fifteenth century, Brunelleschi produced two 'demonstration panels', the Florence Baptistery and the Palazzo Vecchio, showing how correct perspective could be scientifically determined in the depiction of buildings. These have since disappeared and we know about them only through his biography. However, in 1435-6, Alberti, building on the Brunelleschi panels and the work of Donatello and Masaccio, produced a detailed description of perspective technique in his treatise *Della Pittura*. From the 1430s onwards, virtually all the leading Italian painters began to familiarize themselves with perspective. They could thus organize space within their paintings in a natural manner (as seen), and were able to take on in consequence a much greater variety of subjects, and – more important – treat them in far more adventurous and imaginative ways than in the past. The science of perspective was the basis for the art of composition. It is hard to exaggerate the significance of this development in Renaissance painting. It gave artists a freedom they had never enjoyed before.

But many objective difficulties remained, particularly in the materials available to painters and the way in which they had to be used. Late medieval and early Renaissance painters were chiefly employed in covering wall-spaces in churches and palaces, using methods that had been employed in Roman times and almost certainly much earlier. Here we must go into a little technical detail. The Romans smoothed the wall surface and then applied a preliminary layer of lime and sand plaster called (using later Italian painter's terminology) an *arriccio*. If they wished they could then sketch in the outlines of the work (*sinopia*), followed by the application of several layers of lime and powdered marble to give a final smooth surface, or *intonaco*. The paint, a mixture of earth-colours with egg yolk, or tempera, was then applied while the plaster was still wet (a fresco). The paint was then bonded to the wall by the carbonization of the calcium hydroxide in the plaster as it dried. It was the most satisfactory and permanent technique but it involved a great deal of trouble and organization for the painters, who had to work rapidly while the plaster was wet. This often, in large wall-paintings, meant dividing the work into strips corresponding to the height of the scaffolding. If the paint was applied on dry plaster (secco), it was less durable and the surface was more likely to crack and flake. The Romans polished the surface of frescoes, to get a veneer effect, and they also applied wax as a preservative. We know all about this from Pliny's *Natural History* and other sources.

Roman methods of wall-painting never wholly passed out of use in the West, though they lost their complexity and sophistication. From a crude base, then, techniques were gradually improved, rather than revolutionized. In the age of Giotto, the procedure was as follows. The surface was smoothed. Then a rough *arriccio* was applied, one part lime, two parts water. The painter then drew the outlines in charcoal and went over them with a brush to produce the *sinopia*. The entire work was then divided into sections, each one of which could be finished in a day – these were known as *giornate*. Then at the beginning of each day, the allotted portion was covered by the *intonaco*, the outlines were drawn in again, and the painting proceeded. Some bits could then be redone in secco, but with all its disadvantages. The technique is described in detail in Cennino Cennini's treatise, *Il Libro dell'arte*, published about 1390. It has one huge and obvious disadvantage and one less obvious but important advantage. Fresco painting meant you had to take final decisions at an early stage in the work. Once the *sinopia* was complete and measured up, no major changes in composition were possible, and even minor changes raised problems. Spontaneity is ruled out, and as the painter saw his work emerge, he must have been agonized by the faults and misjudgments that emerged too, and he could not correct them, as a rule, without starting all over again. Hence, despite the growing freedom of treatment that artists enjoyed thanks to fore-shortening and perspective techniques, a certain formality and woodenness persisted even in the best work of the early Renaissance.

On the other hand, in Florence in particular, where fresco was always ruthlessly preferred to other methods, artists were forced to think out their projects carefully in advance, and to prepare for them with detailed drawings, of the whole and its parts. This was the great advantage of the system. It made the Florentines concentrate on what they called *disegno*, which embraced both design and draughtsmanship. Florentine artists, or those trained there, thus formed the habit of producing countless drawings, thousands of which survive, and some of them – Raphael's for instance – have become among the greatest treasures of Western art. The drawings were increasingly from life, enabling Florentine artists to observe the human form with fiendish concentration and reproduce it with wonderful fidelity. The glories of the High Renaissance, and its celebration – one might almost say sanctification – of the human body, would have been impossible without this meticulous tradition of draughtsmanship.

All the same, wall-painting in fresco imposed odious limitations on excitable and volatile painters. Mixing pigments with egg yolk has many drawbacks. Some pigments have to be excluded altogether. The paint has to be applied thinly, using delicate hair brushes with a point. It cannot be applied thickly, with *impasto*, and if the artist wants this kind of effect he has to put on repeated layers. He cannot apply the paint smoothly, so that his brushwork becomes invisible, but has to produce a hatched or stippled effect, extraordinarily monotonous on close inspection. He cannot blend or fuse or mix his colours and tones on the surface, which rules out any of those delightful accidental effects that rejoice the heart of every good artist, and which, more important, means that he has to decide in advance exactly what colours he is using in every tiny part of the work. To introduce subtleties and gradations of tone he has to use all kinds of complex techniques. Shadows involve fresh problems, and, in general, attempts at darker effects end in muddiness and despair.

Everything takes a long time, much waiting, and great patience. Of course, as with the preparatory stage, these obstacles provoke forethought, no bad thing for painters, a thoughtless tribe as a rule. They also produce a high palette, and the light colours of the early Renaissance, with a good deal of white or near-white, appeal strongly to many people. On the other hand, the range of colours is narrow and they become tedious in consequence, particularly since they are not mixed or overlaid while painting. This limitation is underlined by the small size of the early Renaissance palette, little more than a narrow oblong, compared to the huge palettes that appeared in the second half of the sixteenth century, when painting with oil had taken over more or less completely. Moreover, not only is the range narrow but the lower, darker tonalities and colours are excluded. Chiaroscuro is ruled out; so is the *sfumato* that Leonardo da Vinci exploited so effectively once he took to oil.

Tempera, then, is not just a different medium to oil, but an inferior one, and it is a fact that, once it passed out of general use, attempts to revive it in the nineteenth and twentieth centuries have never succeeded for long. We come, then, to another central paradox of the Renaissance. Just as, in writing, the most important event of the Renaissance – printing by movable type – was a non-Italian invention, which came from Germany, so in painting, the most welcome technical change of the Renaissance, the adoption of oil for painting, was also a non-Italian development, which came from the Low Countries. (Indeed, you could say that both these discoveries undermine the concept of the Renaissance, since neither was known to antiquity.) We do not get the first reference to mixing pigments with oil until the manual of Theophilus, *De Diversis Artibus*, of 1110–40. Walnut oil or linseed oil was used, and it took an unconscionably long time to dry, as Theophilus complained. The Norwegians used it for altarpieces in the thirteenth century, and they decorated their wooden statues in oil paint. Cennini (1390) sees it as a German method.

However, it was the painters in the Low Countries who took it up in a highly professional way, and improved on the process steadily. By the fifteenth century it was their usual method for painting on panel, and they were beginning to use it on walls too. They quickly discovered that, if you were careful, and placed successive layers of thin oil paint on a detailed underdrawing, you could achieve effects of great translucency and depth, as with stained glass. Indeed, the early oil painters were often glass artists too and learned how to achieve the same glowing effects of church windows on opaque wood surfaces. Dirk Bouts (1415–75) habitually used five layers of thin paint, sometimes more. His contemporary, Jan van Eyck (active 1422–41), achieved results that staggered visitors who had never seen oil employed as a medium – detail, brilliance, sensitivity, great depth and completely new ways of depicting the existence and fall of light. Vasari, writing a hundred years later, was so impressed by Van Eyck's mastery of the medium that he wrongly credited him with inventing it.

Unlike printing, however, painting in oil took a long time to reach Italy and even longer to be generally adopted. Antonello da Messina, a much-travelled painter, is credited with being the first Italian to take it up, and he certainly showed specimens during a visit to Venice in 1475–6. In central Italy, Perugino was using a mixture of oil and tempera in the 1480s, switching entirely to oil during the 1490s. Venice was the first city-school of art to take to oil enthusiastically, and it had lasting effects. It is certainly not true that the Venetians paid little attention to drawing – the two albums that have survived of drawings by Jacopo Bellini, father of Giovanni and Gentile, show how brilliant and inventive Venetian draughtsmen could be. But the Venetians never made a fetish of drawing as the Florentines did, and one reason they adopted oil with such passion was that they could change their minds while at work. X-rays of Giorgione's masterpiece, *The Tempest*, which may be as early as 1505, shows the *pentimenti* that were to become familiar in European art, involving important changes of detail. His collaborator Titian made even more extensive changes and corrections all his life. The Venetians also relished painting in oil because it extended the range of colours open to them, increased their richness and brilliance, and allowed for dramatic contrasting effects of darkness and light. Hence, just as the Florentines were pre-eminent for their draughtsmanship, so the Venetians achieved an unrivalled reputation for colour and drama.

There were other, equally fundamental consequences. If the Dutch and Flemish initially painted in oils on wood, they soon also learned to use stretched canvases, variously treated to receive paint. The introduction of canvas was almost as important as the use of oil, for it gave artists much more freedom in determining the size, shape and texture of their working surface, adding light-ness and economy too. The panel painting, which went back a long time, was succeeded or complemented by the easel painting, which was new and revolutionary. Once an artist could make a living from painting smallish canvases or panels on his easel, he could go in for portraits, then as now one of the most remunerative forms of art; he could either carry his easel about with him or work from his studio – where he could more readily get models, including nude ones, male and female, to sit for him – and above all he could escape from the time-consuming tyranny of the wall-painting. That involved much less church work. Artists continued to create altarpieces in their studios, but this kind of product was now merely one of several. The result was a commercial impetus to the ending of the religious monopoly of art, a process that was taking place anyway but which painting in oils immeasurably accelerated in the sixteenth century. A further result, since the artists escaped from the tyranny of palace walls too, was to break the aristocratic and princely stranglehold on art patronage, and allow the rising bourgeoisie a look-in. This happened much sooner and faster in the Low Countries than elsewhere, but it eventually began to happen in Italy too. To tell the truth, Italian painting was never quite the same after it did.

In addition to these forces of technical change in the world of painting, there was a further fact, more properly belonging to the world of ideas, that was of immense importance in giving the Renaissance its peculiar dynamism. This was the notion of progress. It is of the nature of humankind to wish to improve things and better our condition, and all societies have possessed this wish to some extent. But some societies make it a cardinal principle of existence, whilst others put different considerations first. The ancient Egyptians did not seem to be interested in progress. They were much more anxious to ensure that things were done in the right and canonical way. By contrast, the Greeks sought self-improvement and set targets to be attained, and they spread this notion through their *oikoumene*. They infected the Romans, certainly under the Republic. But under the empire, the authorities became more concerned with order and stability than with advantageous changes. That had a deadening effect on their economy, as we have seen. It also in time affected the arts, which began to regress rather than improve, so that the artistic decadence that we associate with the Dark Ages and the forces of intruding barbarism actually set in well before the empire disintegrated as a defensive system.

Up until the eleventh century, at least, the power of progressive ideas, and the desire to improve systematically on the work of previous generations, was weak. But thereafter it put on strength, and as we have already noted, it drew inspiration from antiquity, when 'they did things so much better than we do'. From the fourteenth century onwards, and especially in Italy, where interest in antiquity was more active, the notion grew that modern men (as they saw themselves) should not only learn all that the ancients had to teach in the days of Rome's glory, but should build on that knowledge to reach even higher standards of knowledge and writing, of architecture, sculpture and art.

What is significant is the way in which the spirit of competition, always strong in Florence, seeking to beat off rivals in Genoa, Venice and elsewhere, spread from commerce to art in the thirteenth century and after. Painters, sculptors and architects were encouraged to compete among themselves for contracts, and still more for glory. As the cult of the individual artist spread, emerging from medieval anonymity to the blaze of personal fame, so the competition sharpened. It was a race within generations and between them.

Dante himself first made the point that Giotto's fame had obscured Cimabue's. Two centuries later Leonardo echoed his remark by affirming, 'He is a wretched pupil who does not surpass his master.' E. H. Gombrich, in a famous essay, 'The Renaissance Conception of Artistic Progress', resurrected a forgotten text of 1473, in which the Florentine humanist Alamanno Rinuccini wrote a dedication to the great artistic patron Federigo da Montefeltro. In it he argued with great force that progress in the arts had been such in recent times that men no longer had to abase themselves before the ancients. He instanced the original work of Cimabue, Giotto and Taddeo Gaddi as being progressively of so high a standard as to make them worthy to stand alongside the artists of the ancient world. Since then, he added, Masaccio had done even better. And what about Domenico Veneziano? And Filippo the Monk (Fra Filippo Lippi)? And John of the Predicant Order (Fra Angelico)? He adds to his litany Ghiberti and Luca della Robbia and, above all, Donatello. Over the whole range of achievements, he insisted, including oratory and the writing of Latin, artists and scholars had been building on the achievements of predecessors to reach standards of performance that had never been equalled in ancient times.

Rinuccini's dedication seems to have been written after he read Alberti's *Della Pittura*. Therein, Alberti stated flatly that his earlier belief – that humanity was in decline and could no longer produce giants like the ancient masters – had been completely dispelled when he returned to Florence and saw the work of Masaccio, Brunelleschi, Donatello, Ghiberti and della Robbia. Artists not only strove to excel each other, let alone their predecessors, but even themselves. And they set up absolute standards taken from the real world they saw around them. Gombrich argues that Ghiberti, perhaps the most conscientious of all the great Renaissance artists, had taken to heart a saying of Lysippus, the finest sculptor of antiquity, which is recorded by Pliny: an artist should not imitate the work of other artists, but nature itself. His second set of bronze doors at the Baptistery were a conscious effort to excel the first, by a closer study of nature. It is likely that men such as Ghiberti and Brunelleschi saw themselves not just as artists but also as scientists (as we would call them), adding by progressive experiments to the sum total of human knowledge. Many of the great paintings of this time were demonstrations of what could be done and how to do it. Patrons knew this, and encouraged it. Each time they commissioned a master, they were striving to help him push forward the frontier of knowledge and skill a little further – or in some cases a lot further. It was the true spirit of the Renaissance.

This, then, is the background against which artists in those days worked. The motion was always forward. There was no turning back. Nor was there stability. But we must not think of painters, at any time during the Renaissance, as prisoners of collective forces. The best of them, particularly, were highly individualistic, laws unto themselves. Cimabue (1240–1302, probable dates), the first of them, set the pattern.

He was known as 'Ox Head'. He was proud, obstinate, highly motivated and absolutely determined to do what he thought right. Dante says that he took no notice of criticism. What Cimabue was trying to do, especially in the frescoes of the sanctuary and crossing at the Upper Church of San Francesco in Assisi, was to absorb all that was valuable in the recent revival of Roman-style art among the Byzantines – new gestures and movements, tones and presentational tricks with vestments and background – while rejecting its suffocating tendency to freeze innovations into canonical devices, and to repeat. The Orthodox Church had a paralysing tendency to tell artists what was the 'correct' way to render holy personages, as well as to limit the range of permitted subjects, something Roman Catholicism did not do until the end of the Council of Trent in 1563. Cimabue fought against this. He was a dramatic man, who painted with great power and sometimes with a touch of the sensational.

This comes through occasionally in his work at Assisi, despite its dreadful condition, which was bad enough even before the earthquake of the 1990s. In the lower walls of the transepts there is a scene of the destruction of Babylon that makes the hair stand on end, and a glorious view of St Mary Magdalen lamenting, an image of grief that alone would differentiate Cimabue from the unadventurous medieval talent that nurtured his genius. He also worked in mosaic, and there is a rendering of St John, in the apse of Pisa Cathedral, which shows a new elegance and sympathy in this stiffest of all techniques, which the Italian artists of the West wisely, as a rule, left to the Byzantines. The difficulty with Cimabue, as with other masters of the early Renaissance, is that their innovations quickly became routine, even clichés, as later artists absorbed and repeated them.

All the same, there was a big leap from Cimabue to Giotto di Bondone (1267–1337), a leap of more than the twenty-seven years that separated their births. Opinion in Italy followed Dante's judgment, and later critics, looking back, saw Giotto as 'the beginning' of something entirely new in painting. Matteo Palmieri, writing in the 1430s, referred to painting 'before Giotto' as 'the lifeless mistress of laughable figures'. It was 'full of amazing stupidities' before Giotto 'resurrected' it. We see in the best portions of his work in the Arena Chapel at Padua (1303–6), the *Lamentation*, for instance, the *Betrayal of Christ* and *Joachim and the Shepherds*, the emergence of genuine pictures as we understand them today, with figures intelligently and skilfully grouped, located clearly in space and in surroundings that bear some resemblance to the actual world. In *Joachim* the trees are absurd and the sheep are rat-like, but the dog is real and the shepherds are people one can actually see tending their flocks on the hillside. Both the *Betrayal* and the *Lamentation* convey deep intensity of feeling, expressed in anxious, convulsed and tearful faces which one recognizes from the streets and the fields of common life. Two decades later, in the Bardi and the Peruzzi Chapels at Santa Croce in Florence, and possibly in the Upper Church at Assisi, Giotto was painting his figures with greater freedom and facility – they have grace as well as motion – and he placed them within increasingly complex perspective settings, so that there is considerable depth within the composition. For the first time since antiquity, the onlooker can step into the scene and feel at home there. Giotto's work has fared better than Cimabue's but his later masterpieces, which were the ones that most impressed his contemporaries and successors, have not survived. Later artists tended to place him at the head of the apostolic succession of great painters, who had annihilated the Byzantine manner and made nature his model – this last is a point that Ghiberti, Alberti and Leonardo all made in their comments on his work.

Looking back from the vantage point of the mid-sixteenth century, Vasari divided the development of art into three periods, the first introduced by Giotto, the second by Masaccio, the third by Leonardo. There is some truth in this but it is not the whole truth. The common opinion among artists, at any rate by the mid-fifteenth century, was that Giotto's followers and successors failed to improve materially on his performance because they neglected the study of nature. Masaccio, coming more than half a century later, 'restored' his work and improved upon it. Hence he is often seen as the first great Renaissance painter, though in justice to Giotto, he ought to be called the second. Unlike Giotto, who was a harbinger of the Renaissance, Masaccio was a beneficiary of it:

he was aware of the classical texts on painting; he knew far more about the recovered literature; he was infused with the spirit of antiquity in a way that was impossible in the early fourteenth century. More important, perhaps, he benefited both from the perspective work of Brunelleschi and the figure rendering of Donatello. In effect his entire working life was less than a decade, and much of it has been lost. But, thanks to the outstanding sculptors among whom he worked, he did two things that were beyond Giotto. First, in for instance the central panel of an altarpiece, *Virgin and Child*, now in the National Gallery, London, and still more in the *Trinity* fresco in Santa Maria Novella, Florence, he made his perspective settings look natural, something he had clearly learned from intense study of Brunelleschi's demonstration panels. Second, in his beautiful panel *St Paul*, from the Pisa altarpiece, he produced a genuine three-quarter-length portrait-study of the saint, painted with wonderful facility, the face and hands rendered with grace, sensitivity and confidence. The influence of Donatello's figure-statues is transparent, but Masaccio adds a softness and sympathy that the fierce Donatello lacks. The same spirit infuses the beautiful fresco, *Tribute Money*, which Masaccio painted on the wall of the Brancacci Chapel in the Florentine Chapel of Santa Maria del Carmine. Figures, houses and background mountains do not blend with the perfection of nature. But the artist is almost there. This was painted in 1427, nearly a century after Giotto's best work; and it shows that a great deal had been learned in those hundred years. It is not surprising that Alberti almost certainly had Masaccio in mind as the model painter of the age (1436), though by then he had been dead eight years.

Indeed, with the passing of Masaccio it becomes impossible to see Italian painting simply as an apostolic succession. So much by now had been learned, and so many had learned it, that art was branching out in different, sometimes rival and even contradictory directions. The new freedom conveyed by knowledge, to place realistic figures in convincing space, allowed individual artists to develop their own personalities with an energy and imagination that had been impossible before 1420.

There was, for instance, Paolo Uccello, who was a little older than Masaccio and who lived a great deal longer, 1397–1475. He developed a lifelong fascination for perspective, and acquired a remarkable mastery of it. He loved foreshortening to the point of frenzy, and geometry as a science as well as an art. Nature he was much less interested in, however, though he was lucky enough to work under Ghiberti. His three great panels, *The Battle of San Romano*, now split up and in Paris, Florence and London, are almost a demonstration, like Brunelleschi's panels, of the techniques of perspective and foreshortening. But the knights look like toy soldiers, riding rocking-horses, and the battleground is a floor rather than a field. Yet the images are memorable, indeed stunning, and there is an engrossing charm in the best of Uccello's work, such as the *Hunting Scene* in the Oxford Ashmolean. It is not nature: it is art, of a highly individual kind. Uccello was a medieval painter in some ways, striving for patterned, decorative effects rather than the humanistic purity of line which the tradition of Giotto represented, and which Masaccio embodied.

The decorative impulse was strong, not least because so many patrons relished it. In the 1420s the Venetian painter Gentile da Fabriano (1385–1427) was brought to Florence by the head of the Strozzi banking family to create a magnificent altarpiece for their private chapel. The central panel, *The Adoration of the Magi*, is one of the jewels of the Renaissance – almost literally, for it glitters with gold and sumptuous filigree-work, reminding us again that many painters started off in jewellers' workshops and used paint to produce for their patrons huge, two-dimensional jewels to hang on their walls, the sacred subject-matter being an antidote to luxurious worldliness. The three kings, with their scintillating garments, gave Gentile an excuse for a virtuoso display of his technique. But this glorious painting, which delights us as much as it clearly pleased contemporaries – it was widely influential – is also an exercise in perspective, as the royal procession meanders away into the distance, and in lighting, which is brilliantly rendered and highly naturalistic. There is another factor. Though the principal figures are idealized, the crowd of courtiers and followers behind them are, as it were, picked out from the streets of Florence and the canals of Venice, a wonderful collection of faces drawn from life in the third decade of the fifteenth century, coarse, shrewd, cunning, curious, smug and happy – the physiognomy of life.

This interest in people, who could be fitted into the demands of religious iconography, became a salient characteristic of Renaissance painting. Fra Filippo Lippi (c. 1406–69) was an orphan, brought up in a convent, who was persuaded to take vows and then caused an immense scandal by running off with a nun. The Medici family, who had already recognized his talent, intervened to get him laicized, and the child born to the couple, Filippino Lippi (1457–1504), also became a highly successful painter. Filippo's majestic frescoes in the cathedrals of Spoleto and Prato gave him the opportunity to paint some splendid crowd scenes. His Madonnas and saints are holy, serene and unworldly, but his crowds are common clay, men and women as he saw them. There is the same dichotomy in his contemporary, Fra Angelico (c. 1395–1455), who painted the Virgin and Child with impressive tenderness and holy simplicity (though with sumptuous colour effects). His ability to inspire devotion brought him a multitude of ecclesiastical clients. Though a Dominican friar by vocation, he ran the busiest workshop in Florence, and was eventually summoned to Rome to work for the popes. Yet every face he painted is that of an individual character. His *St Peter Preaching* (1433), part of what is known as the Linaiuoli Tabernacle (now in the San Marco Museum, Florence), shows a group of people, each wrapped in his or her own thoughts – none actually listening to the sermon – as though all were sitting for portraits. There is a closely observed group of beggars, in *St Lawrence Distributing Alms* (1448), in the Vatican, which shows the same determined grasp of personality. But it has to be said that St Lawrence's splendid vestments are a work of art in themselves, and the architectural background, rendered in dazzling perspective and ornate detail, demonstrates other Renaissance obsessions, which preoccupied the saintly Angelico as much as they did more mundane practitioners of the art. Behind the new Renaissance sophistication, there is often a hint of medieval childishness.

That is particularly apparent in the masterpiece of Fra Angelico's most gifted pupil, Benozzo Gozzoli (c. 1420–97), whose *Journey of the Magi* (1459–61) occupies three walls of the Chapel of the Medici in their Florentine *palazzo*. This is more than a repeat of Gentile's *Magi*, though clearly inspired by it, for there are three separate processions, one for each king, all presented in sumptuous detail, in gold, vermilion, purple and olive green – and a variety of other colours – meandering through fields and towns, with camels, horses, asses, mules and dogs, leopards chasing deer, birds and flowers, exotic trees and castles, all done to astonish and dazzle. Many of those presented in the processions are portraits of Medici family members and their followers, and there is a head of Benozzo himself. This room, which has other works by Benozzo in its sanctuary, is one of the finest achievements of the Renaissance, for the frescoes, now restored, are well preserved and near enough to the visitor for the details to be relished. No one who has been in this enchanting room is likely to forget it. It is Renaissance religious entertainment at its innocent best, a celebration of the joy of living in a world of beauty and fun.

A similar, but far more formidable work in Mantua, the *Camera degli Sposi*, of Andrea Mantegna (1430–1506), finished in 1474, indicates the rapid progress that Italian painting was now making, and also the difference between an accomplished artist of the second rank, like Gozzoli, and a great master. Mantegna was a difficult man and a slow worker, for nearly half a century the court painter to the Gonzagas of Mantua, who coped with his shortcomings in saintly manner. (One of the sources of Renaissance strength, it is worth repeating, was the willingness of proud princes to submit to the artistic temperament.) He had worked in Padua, where he met Donatello, then creating his great equestrian statue, and learned from him not only the secrets of Florentine scientific artistry but his passion for character seen in the raw. Perhaps he should have been a sculptor: the man who taught him painting, Francesco Squarcione, criticized his painted figures for looking as if they were made of marble or stone. His famous *Dead Christ*, now in Milan, a daring exercise in foreshortening, looks as if it was carved with a chisel rather than painted with a brush, and his autobiographical *Presentation in the Temple*, showing – so legend has it – his own wife and their first-born, though done in tempera on canvas, is as solid as granite. In Mantegna's grand altarpieces, like the *Crucifixion* in the Louvre and the *Agony in the Garden* in London's National Gallery, the figures seem to spring out of, and be anchored in, the rock on which they are placed. Their petrification gives them an awesome presence, as though they were harder as well as larger than life, and there is an undertone of terror and fear in some of Mantegna's religious imagery that hints at the wrath of God. He was one of the most learned of Renaissance artists, an expert on Rome, its architecture, its decorative motifs and its armour and weaponry, and his strong historical sense led him to present his scenes from the Bible against an antique background authentic in every detail – thus distancing his superhuman figures still more from everyday fifteenth-century life.

Yet the *Camera degli Sposi* is an equally authentic presentation of fifteenth-century court life, as the painter actually witnessed it in the palace of the Gonzagas. The two main scenes, one outdoors (*The Meeting*), one indoors (*The Signing of the Contract*), take us straight into the world of ceremony, diplomacy, intrigue and manoeuvring later described in words by Machiavelli and Castiglione. Indeed, in some ways these paintings, one in fresco, one largely in secco, tell us rather more about Renaissance courts than either of the two standard texts. There are many marvellous things in this room, including an eye or painted lunette in the ceiling which introduces the new technique of *di sotto in sù* whereby figures are deliberately distorted to look natural when seen from the ground looking up – something Mantegna worked out from a typical Donatello trick. It prefigures the work of Correggio in the next generation and, indeed, the whole of the Baroque. Yet there are no tricks about the figures. These are actual faces of real people – fifteenth-century Italians of the urban, courtly breed, whispering and hiding their thoughts, making honeyed speeches, dissimulating and orating, boasting and cutting a *bella figura*, strutting for effect and feigning every kind of emotion – the women less numerous but more cunning than the men. The vicious-looking dogs are authentic too, and castles, houses, churches and countryside vividly depict the north of Italy. As in all Mantegna's work, one learns a great deal because, though a master of illusionistic devices, he always tells the truth.

Mantegna's interest in landscape, and the fidelity with which he presented it, underlines his northern Italian origins. If Florentine art had a weakness, it was that it focussed too exclusively on the human body. The architectural settings in which it placed the figures were props or exercises in perspective, rather than observed realities with their own intrinsic interest. The further north one gets, the more the forests and mountains, valleys and rivers impinge, and the towns are real ones, minutely recorded, rather than abstractions. Venice, though a powerful, rich and hyperactive city with a long tradition of artistic patronage, was slow to acquire the Renaissance spirit. It had nothing like Florence's apostolic succession of Cimabue, Giotto and Masaccio. But from the second quarter of the fifteenth century, it began to produce great paintings, thanks mainly to the brilliant Bellini family. Its patriarch Jacopo Bellini (c. 1400–71), married his daughter Nicolosia to Mantegna, and (though the son of a pewterer) was himself taught by Gentile da Fabriano – so we have here one of the most densely woven artistic networks of the period.

Jacopo is known chiefly through his marvellous albums of drawings in the Louvre and the British Museum, but his son Gentile Bellini (c. 1429–1507) was a Venetian court painter of eminence who used the Venetian background to great effect in his work. His *Miracle of the True Cross at San Lorenzo* is a superb urban landscape, in which the buildings, painted in the most minute detail, tulip-chimneys and all, are the chief characters. Indeed, as an artist of townscape, he was surpassed only by his pupil, the great Vittore Carpaccio (c. 1460–1525), whose many identifiable Venetian backgrounds, including the marshes and lagoons as well as the city itself, make him one of the most fascinating realists of the entire Renaissance. Carpaccio was particularly ingenious at introducing dogs into his townscapes and interiors, as in his delightful painting of St Augustine in his study, a beautifully observed depiction of the kind of room, with all its equipment, in which humanist scholars worked. Dogs also figure in his notable rendering of two Venetian ladies watching events from a balcony. Gentile Bellini, however, capped this by exotic touches, garnered during what seem to have been extensive travels in the eastern Mediterranean. In his giant painting, *St Mark Preaching in Alexandria*, not only camels but a giraffe figure, and there are touches of Arab architecture (plus a self-portrait wearing a gold chain presented to him by the Sultan). His *Procession of the True Cross in the Piazza San Marco* shows the façade of the basilica, a major topographical work of art and a reminder that Canaletto sprang from a long Venetian tradition which was 250 years old when he was born.

Giovanni Bellini (c. 1431–1516), Gentile's brother, never travelled outside the Veneto during his long life – Vasari says he was ninety when he died – and seems to have had a passionate attachment to its scenery, which peeps out behind and sometimes towers over the figures in his sacred altarpieces and other paintings. It is often a rustic landscape, with farmers working their fields and cattle browsing. It has echoes of Netherlandish work, going back to the Limburg brothers of the early fifteenth century, whose *Très Riches Heures du Duc de Berry,* the most sumptuous Book of Hours produced at the close of the Middle Ages, depicts all the agricultural seasons in turn. Though untravelled, Bellini lived in one of the busiest crossroads of Europe, and was exposed to Dutch, Flemish, German and French works, as well as Florentine and Lombard influences. He absorbed and transmuted them all into a highly personal and distinctive style which nonetheless constantly progressed as his skills, always formidable, developed, and his interests expanded. He was at the centre of the technical revolutions that made painting in oil dominant, introduced the easel painting and made portraiture popular. He had a wonderful eye for a face, and huge skill at getting it down on panel or canvas, while at the same time his renderings of the Madonna and her Child made bishops and canons flock to employ him. He dignified the doges, brought tears to the eyes of elderly abbesses, and applied prodigies of inventiveness and imagination to renderings of hackneyed subjects, like the *Pietà*, the *Drunkenness of Noah*, the *Repentant Magdalen* and *St John the Baptist*.

Giovanni Bellini drew with all the grace of his father, but brought his paintings up to a high finish that delighted all. He had sensitivity and delicacy, making his women seem the essence of tenderness. There are many charming touches, such as the boy instrumentalists seated at the foot of the Virgin's throne in his San Giobbe altarpiece (Accademia, Venice), a device imitated by many later artists. Indeed, they plundered all his ideas, and tried, many unsuccessfully, to copy his virtuoso technique. He ran a huge studio, with dozens of assistants, attracted by his fame from all over the region, and it is likely that masters as diverse as Titian, Sebastiano del Piombo and Lorenzo Lotto passed through his shop at an early stage in their careers. At the beginning of the sixteenth century, he was widely regarded as the greatest living painter, known throughout Europe. Yet he continued to absorb new ideas and influences, including the young Giorgione, from the next generation but one. Dürer, in Venice in 1506 when Bellini was in his late seventies, said he was painting as well as ever, 'still the best'. Bellini has always been fervently admired by painters themselves and those with a passionate interest in art, like Ruskin, who declared his altarpiece in San Zaccaria and his triptych in the Venice Frari the two finest paintings in the world.

The rise of a mature school of painting in Venice was characteristic of the spread of the fine arts all over Italy during the fifteenth century. Piero della Francesca (c. 1415–92) worked on high-quality commissions in towns all over central Italy, such as Perugia and Arezzo, where his fresco-cycle of *The Legend of the True Cross* constitutes his most considerable work. He illustrates the extraordinary lust for learning that the Renaissance bred, and the upward progression of its artists. For his father was a tanner and his own first job was to paint the striped poles used to carry candles in religious processions. Yet he made himself a master-mathematician and played a bigger role in reviving and spreading the use of Euclid than anyone else. Three of his innumerable learned treatises survive, including his *De prospectiva pingendi*, an exposition of the rules of perspective that demanded more mathematical knowledge than most painters have ever possessed. Perspective figured in his paintings sometimes to the exclusion of other, more central requirements and to the confusion of the public. Thus in his wonderfully light and radiant *Flagellation*, in the Ducal Palace, Urbino, Christ and his assailants have been pushed backstage while three unrelated figures, who are not even watching the scourging, dominate the foreground. Piero was an eccentric. In his *Baptism of Christ* in the National Gallery, London, interest is as likely to centre on the man taking his shirt off, or the three shocked angels, as on the Baptist pouring Jordan water on Christ's head. The *Resurrection*, in Piero's home town of Sansepolcro, is an amazing work, with Christ emerging somnabulistically from a marble sarcophagus against which the sleepers lie. There is about all Piero's characterizations – saints, singers, onlookers, dignitaries – a certain icy calm, a frozen stillness, which perhaps reflects his obsession with that chilly science, geometry. Yet he has an extraordinary gift for planting his images on one's mind, indissolubly, which after all is the mark of a great painter. This ability may explain why he, together with Sandro Botticelli (1445–1510), today constitute, for most people, the very essence of the Italian Renaissance.

Botticelli was an eccentric too, and like Piero (who was thirty years older) a passionate humanist, though his interests were literary rather than scientific. Where Piero was static, Botticelli was fluid, sinuous, dynamic, with a strong, elastic line, so that his figures are drawn onto the surface rather than built up out of it. They sway, they dance, they wreath themselves into undulating patterns, interwoven with flowers and trees, sea, sand and grass. Botticelli was the first great Renaissance artist to make full use of ancient mythology not merely for subject-matter – *The Birth of Venus*, *Primavera*, *et al.* – but to give his works spiritual content. There is a daring whiff of paganism about his blonde maidens and goddesses, an insouciance, a hedonism and a cool, bold, graceful sensuality – never lascivious or carnal – that is overwhelmingly attractive, now as it undoubtedly was then. But Botticelli was also a prolific and efficient producer of Virgins and Baby Jesuses – some of them even better than those of his master, Filippo Lippi – and he was in constant employment for the churches, as well as the palaces of the Medici, who preferred the pagan work. He may, indeed, have been a man of strong religious bent at times, for when the fierce Dominican friar Girolamo Savonarola (1452–98) began to preach (initially at Lorenzo de' Medici's invitation) against worldly vanities, and begged the population to burn rich dresses, scandalous books and unholy pictures, Botticelli is said to have responded, and burned some of his own works (it is true that some of those whose existence we know of from literary sources have vanished). When Sixtus IV, having built his Sistine Chapel, brought artists to Rome to decorate the lower part of its walls, Botticelli was one of those chosen (1481) and contributed *The Temptation of Christ* and episodes from the *Life of Moses*, not with any great success. Paganism was his forte and myth his inspiration. But artists do not always know what is good for them.

The second half of the fifteenth century was an exceptional period of busy activity and the nurturing of genius in Florence. There were those who pursued an individual path, like Piero di Cosimo (1462–1521); he loved painting animals, drew well from nature and made a speciality of depicting his own wild interpretations of mythology. He was one of the few Florentines who loved landscape and his weird *Death of Procris* in London's National Gallery, with its desolate estuary, magnificent dog (and other creatures) and its long-eared faun, combines his obsessions. He made his living designing magnificent banners and other gear for public ceremonies but he was by nature a loner, who left the busy studio of Cosimo Rosselli, his guardian, as soon as he could work on his own. Vasari says he was a recluse, who lived off hard-boiled eggs, pre, ring them fifty at a time while boiling his glue for size. He loathed noise, especially crying children, church music, old men coughing and flies buzzing. But at one time or another he taught, and inspired, a number of remarkable painters, including Fra Bartolommeo (c. 1472–1517), Andrea del Sarto (1486–1530) and Jacopo Pontormo (1494–1556).

Most Florentine art, however, revolved round the large workshops. There was that run by the Pollaiuolo family, chiefly Antonio (1432–98) and his brother Piero (1441–96). Antonio was trained as a goldsmith and practised the craft. He also made superb bronze statuettes, designed embroidery and produced stained glass. Both brothers painted. Together they created the gigantic *Martyrdom of Saint Sebastian*, one of the glories of the National Gallery in London, which is really a brilliant exercise in the presentation of the nude or semi-clothed male. Antonio's preoccupation with the nude is further illustrated in his remarkable engraving *The Battle of the Ten Nudes*. Medieval artists had kept well clear of nudity, except for damned souls in Hell, but it now became a subject in which Florentine artists, with their strict tradition of draughtsmanship, specialized. Not only did they draw from the nude (males only; women, except prostitutes, willing to pose nude were rare) but in Antonio's case studied anatomy too. It was one way in which the Renaissance passion for exact, scientific knowledge expressed itself. A large workshop, like the Pollaiuolos', not only employed models regularly but kept stocks of anatomical casts in plaster – arms, feet, torsos, etc – for rapid copying. The brothers did a lot of drawing and engraving, as well as producing ceremonial material and banners for tournaments, and Piero in particular experimented in painting in oils on panel, playing a notable part in making it the standard medium in Tuscany.

A much bigger workshop was run by the Ghirlandaios, Domenico (1449–94) and Davide (1452–1525). They came from a background of agile craftsmen working in leather, cloth, tapestry and other decorative soft goods, and employed numerous members of their family, sons, in-laws and so forth. Domenico's was the organizing, businesslike brain. Though he occasionally worked in Rome, on for instance the lower range of the Sistine Chapel frescoes, he spent most of his life producing a mass of high-quality artistic goods. These included mosaics, something the Florentines usually left to Venice. He painted a grand series of frescoes for Santa Maria Novella in Florence, which are remarkable for their durability. Domenico took *buon fresco* extremely seriously and practised this difficult craft with highly professional polish, which explains the strong survival-power of his output. He also drew beautifully in true local fashion, and large numbers of his drawings have come down to us, so that we can see exactly how a conscientious Florentine artist-craftsman built up a finished picture. He was indeed the epitome of all that was meticulous and professional in Florentine art in the broadest sense, always striving to excel himself and experimenting with new media and techniques. These included various mixtures of oil and tempera, brush-tip drawing, chalk, pen and ink and metalpoint for drawings, with white highlights, and brush drawings on prepared linen. Vasari lists many artists who were trained in Domenico's shop, including Michelangelo, whose early drawings at least strongly reflect the technique of his master.

The most famous shop of all, however – as we have already noticed – was Verrocchio's. This was a powerhouse of ideas and a brilliant seminary of a huge variety of techniques in different media, for Verrocchio was an all-round craftsman and his figure-sculpture and bronze-casting were particularly fine. His most famous assistant was Leonardo da Vinci (1452–1519) who was there several years and learned a lot not only from the master but from other brilliant pupils. His training helps to explain the extraordinary breadth of his interests. However, we must not take too elevated a view of the Florentine art-shop. It was a business venture, whose chief object was to get lucrative commissions, execute them at a profit, and excel or fend off the competition. Florence was about art. But it was also about money, and it was the peculiar gift of leading Florentine craftsmen to pursue one without allowing the other to suffer. In Verrocchio's shop, the craftsmanship had to be faultless – he insisted on that – but every aid to efficient production was ruthlessly adopted. We see this in Verrocchio's *Tobias and the Angel*, now in London's National Gallery, his exemplary response to a competitive work by the Pollaiuolo brothers on the same, highly popular subject. Their painting is altogether delightful – nothing illustrates better the freshness and joy of the Renaissance – but it is trade all the same. It now seems likely that Verrocchio himself only painted the Angel, as the principal figure, and left Tobias to the young Leonardo. And Leonardo also did all four hands, the two left hands, which are identical, being drawn from studio casts (the right hands are a bit suspicious too). None of this detracts from the excellence of the work, but it is a reminder that, in fifteenth-century Florence, there was a continuum from the counting house, through the wholesale cloth warehouse, to shops selling embroidery and coloured shoes, to the all-purpose art-workshop, catering for the sometimes vulgar taste of rich parvenus but also producing works of genius that we now venerate.

Verrocchio was an organized man. Leonardo was not. He was an intellectual, more interested in ideas than people. He came from a background of well-to-do Tuscan notaries, though he was illegitimate and brought up by grandparents in a large extended family. We do not know much about his education, but it was clearly extensive, and in Verrocchio's shop he was well trained to make his living in a variety of ways. Leonardo's gifts were enormous, and nobody ever doubted them, at the time or since. He was the universal man, the epitome of the questing spirit of the Renaissance and its desire to excel in every possible way. As he grew older, people held him in awe: he was the sage, the magus, the Man of Genius. He was also difficult to work with, or employ. His weaknesses were twofold, and they were important.

Leonardo was interested in every aspect of the visible world – his earliest surviving work is a brilliant Tuscan landscape drawing – and he was fascinated by the varieties of nature, above all by the human body in all its forms and moods. But he was interested in these things as phenomena, and viewed them with scientific detachment. There was not much warmth to him. He may, indeed, have had homosexual inclinations, for in 1476, when he was twenty-four, he was accused of sodomy, though this does not necessarily imply the practice of unnatural vice (the accusation was anonymous and nothing came of it).

Moreover, although Leonardo's interest in the human body was paramount, as befitted a Renaissance humanist–artist, his huge range of other preoccupations – with weather and waves, animals and vegetation and scenery, machines of all kinds but especially weapons of war and fortifications, all of them expressed in elaborate drawings as well as expounded in his *Notebooks* – meant that his time and energy were thinly spread. His priorities were unclear. No one can say for sure whether he regarded painting an easel portrait like the *Mona Lisa*, or the *Last Supper* wall-painting in Milan, or designing an impregnable fortress, as the thing he most wanted to do, or was most worth doing.

Furthermore, with such a range of interests, he lacked the ferocious concentration on any particular one, at any one time, which his younger contemporary, Michelangelo, could bring to bear. As we have seen, Michelangelo sometimes left things unfinished. Leonardo was a much more extreme case of the distracted and ill-disciplined polymath. As early as 1478, when he was still working in Verrocchio's shop, he was given a personal commission to do an altarpiece in a chapel off the Piazza della Signoria. But he never got round to it or never seriously began work, and Filippino

Lippi had to be called in to carry it out. No one who saw anything done by him, even a mere drawing, failed to admire him, and he was in constant demand by the mightiest patrons, from leading Florentines to the Sforzas of Milan, Pope Leo X and kings Louis XII and François I of France. But this glittering career is punctuated by rows over intolerable delays, disputes over money, presumably arising from his unbusinesslike methods, and repetitive simple failures to do what he had promised. He was not in the least lazy, as some artists are, or tiresomely perfectionist. But the final public output was meagre. There are only ten surviving paintings that are generally accepted as his. Three others are unfinished. Yet more were completed by other artists.

It is true that, at his finished best, Leonardo produced work of the very highest quality, interest and originality. Opinion may remain divided over the *Mona Lisa*, a portrait he worked on over many years and which shows the defects of his slovenly method of working – the face, and the hands, are woefully inconsistent – or the London National Gallery's *Virgin of the Rocks*, which also had a long and distracted history. The *Virgin and Child with St Anne and a Lamb*, in the Louvre, likewise has its critics as well as a host of admirers. Yet the *Portrait of a Lady with an Ermine* (1490), an oil on panel now in Cracow, Poland, is as close to perfection as a painting can well be: beautifully composed and full of fascination – the woman was a favourite mistress of his Sforza patron – it combines charm, dignity, indeed majesty and mystery in equal proportions. The right hand, and the exquisite creature it is stroking, are painted with a decisive skill that testifies to Leonardo's patient devotion to nature, and the gaze of the girl, enigmatic as always with Leonardo, is unforgettable.

Yet the fact remains that this panel is one of the rare occasions that a patron got what he had ordered. Leonardo's reputation for non-delivery – as one pope put it: 'Leonardo? Oh, he is the man who does not finish things' – was compounded by his passion for experiment, which produced disasters of a different kind but equally infuriating to those who paid. The Sforzas asked him to paint scenes on the walls of the refectory of Santa Maria delle Grazie in Milan, and he actually completed the *Last Supper*, which was instantly admired for its highly original composition and the striking interest of the faces. But his experimental techniques led to its rapid deterioration, and the other scenes never emerged. Other ambitious wall-scenes, in Milan and Florence, came to nothing; or little has survived. On the other hand, Leonardo produced a design for the crossing-tower of Milan Cathedral, worked on a huge bronze equestrian statue, accepted the appointment of 'architect and general engineer' to the ruffianly warlord Cesare Borgia, and produced various large-scale cartoons, one of which survives, for projected paintings. He worked on muscular power, optics, hydraulics, articulated flying machines, bastions and siege engines, facial expressions and human psychology, all of these preoccupations being lavishly illustrated in notebooks and detached sheets. The comparison with Coleridge is irresistible: notes took the place of finished work. As with Piero della Francesca, Leonardo's interest in geometry grew. It was, perhaps, the dominant theme of the last years of his life, though he also seems to have dwelt obsessively on the prospects of catastrophic storms and other extreme weather conditions. These years were spent in or near the French court, where François I became his ideal patron: reverential, generous, unharassing, content merely to have in attendance this great Italian seer, who could do so many remarkable things when he chose, and whose conversation was a Renaissance in itself.

Leonardo's influence on his immediate successors or near-contemporaries, including Raphael, was immense, both in organizing large-scale painting and in painting techniques. He wrote extensively on painting, though nothing was actually published until the mid-seventeenth century. But his views were known – that, for instance, 'correct' mathematical perspective did not actually produce what we think we see, and required correction. Where the Greeks used a special curvature or *entasis*, Leonardo blurred outlines, a technique that came to be known as *sfumato*, and which the adoption of oil-painting made highly effective. He was therefore behind the shift away from the strong outlines preferred in the fifteenth century, of which Botticelli, for example, made such brilliant use, to the rounded, more painterly techniques of the sixteenth century, involving a large degree of shadowing, the systematic use of highlights, and chiaroscuro.

This was one of the most significant and lasting innovations in the history of Western painting. Leonardo also introduced, or at any rate made famous, the practice of drawing in black and sanguine chalk, often with white highlights, on various shades of paper. Thousands of artists made use of it after him, often with spectacular results. Leonardo's influence was progressive and cumulative, as prints that he inspired were published, his drawings circulated, and the texts of his writings gradually became available. It is hard to think of any artist of stature who has been impervious to his work. Hence, despite the unsatisfactory state of his output at his death, he has been regarded as the founder of the period known as the High Renaissance, in the years around the turn of the fifteenth-sixteenth centuries, when the progress of the movement to restore and excel antiquity came to a climax at the highest level of achievement, and with the greatest impact on the future.

If Leonardo encompassed the Renaissance intellectually, Raphael or Raffaello Sanzio (1483–1520) epitomized its quest for beauty and its success in finding it. For if his life was short (he died when only thirty-seven) his output was large, continuous, invariably of the highest possible quality, and finished. Patrons found him the perfect painter: affable, reliable, always doing what he said he would do and delivering on time. He ran what became a large studio efficiently, using his assistants intelligently and in ways that were fair both to them and to patrons. He was born in that leading centre of culture, Urbino, but trained in Perugia, under Pietro Vanucci or Perugino as he was known (c. 1446–1525). Perugino was a product of the Verrocchio shop and of the college of painters that Sixtus IV set up to do the lower walls of his Sistine Chapel. He had a sentimental eye and a lush contour but he could paint a lovable Madonna and an elevating saint as well as anyone else of his generation, and he taught the young Raphael most of what he knew. It says a lot for Raphael's aesthetic and emotional integrity, and cool, calm taste, that he avoided all Perugino's faults while absorbing his undoubted strengths, and building on them.

Raphael's work falls into two main categories: the large-scale frescoes and decorative work that he did for the Vatican Palace at the direction of Pope Julius II, and his devotional easel works and altarpieces mainly of the Virgin and Child, sometimes with minor figures. He did a few portraits too, especially a masterly presentation of Castiglione, which has taught generations of portraitists how to set about it. His range, then, was selective, though it should be added that he succeeded Bramante as architect of St Peter's, was a decorator of genius, and was also branching out into new directions in painting at the time of his sudden death.

With Raphael, what you see is what you get. His paintings in the Vatican, such as *The School of Athens*, are intelligent, large-scale organizations of superbly painted figures, which have guided 'history painters', as they call themselves, throughout Europe from the sixteenth to the late nineteenth century. There are no obscurities or mysteries, no hidden meanings, no ambiguities, no shocks, no nastiness, no horror, no thrills. There is not much to be said about them except that they are extremely good of their kind. His Madonnas are rather different. They too contain no hidden agendas or *arrière-pensées*, no adumbrations of Freudianism, nothing indeed for modern academics to get their suspicious teeth into. On the other hand, they are a wonderfully inventive set of variations on a theme that is absolutely central to Western religious art. They do exactly what they set out to do: to inspire devotion in the religious-minded, and rapture in the aesthete. These Madonnas are real, living women, who are also queens of heaven, painted with astonishing skill, never repetitious, without the smallest hint of vulgarity, always serene and tender, devoted and reverent. Julius II summoned Raphael to Rome to do God's work in paint, and that is just what he did, supplying through copies and prints the devotional decoration for the walls of countless convents, seminaries, presbyteries and Catholic colleges from that day to this. They are familiar enough to risk boring us but never actually do so, and to study these noble paintings from close to, as they still exist after half a millennium, is to appreciate what enduring art is all about.

There was, however, one additional element in Raphael's art that does not fit neatly into this picture of superb and decorous proficiency. A part of Raphael rejected serenity and sought transcendence. One of his Vatican frescoes, *Fire in the Borgo* (c. 1515), presents terror and anarchy, and the mob appealing for a miracle.

Raphael was a materialist who longed to believe in the supernatural, and in this sense regretted the medieval world, with its absolute credulity, which was now slipping away. Medieval painters could present the supernatural, and did it all the time. But they could not convey it by painterly techniques of atmospheric light and subtle suggestiveness. Raphael could. Normally he did not choose to do so. His Madonnas and 'Sacred Conversations', with saints posed together in seemly adoration of the divine, are tender and elevating but stick to nature. However, in the *Sistine Madonna* (now in Dresden), Raphael depicts a Virgin and Child of astonishing beauty, and absolutely solid and real, who nevertheless are not of this world and seem to be levitating upwards by supernatural power, poised between earth and heaven. It is the painting of a vision, and astonishingly successful.

Raphael follows this trend in his magnificent last painting, the huge *Transfiguration*, completed in the year he died, 1520, and now in the Vatican Museum. Christ floats above the astonished apostles, realistically painted but a mass of light and air, while at the bottom of the picture a scene of chaos shows his disciples trying and failing to cure a frantic boy whom daemons have seized. It is not surprising that this work awed contemporaries and made them ponder. It hints of a new world of art to come, and makes the tragedy of Raphael's early death seem even more poignant.

The 'divine trio' of the High Renaissance, Leonardo, Raphael and Michelangelo, whilst of different ages, were all alive and working at the same time, and there must have been interactions between their powerful artistic personalities, though this is largely conjecture. The impact of Leonardo can be clearly traced in many of Raphael's superb drawings. He adopted red chalk and replaced the boy or male models he used for female figures (a practice also followed by Michelangelo) by women models, and the results are spectacular. They ravished young artists at the time, for Raphael was generous and open in showing work in progress to his colleagues, and they have inspired emulation in the greatest figure-painters ever since. Raphael's relationship with Michelangelo, on the other hand, was different. They were both working in Rome together. There is no evidence that Raphael was ever jealous of a fellow artist – quite the contrary – but Michelangelo was introspective and secretive and could be mean-minded. His friend Sebastiano del Piombo (1485–1547), also in Rome from 1511 and a considerable painter in his own right, used to feed Michelangelo with anti-Raphael anecdotes, presumably because the master wished to hear them.

The difficulty for Michelangelo, in his relations with Raphael, is that he considered himself, and was, primarily a sculptor. He painted little before he came to Rome to produce his three great series of frescoes (the Sistine Chapel ceiling; the *Last Judgment* of the altar end-wall; and the Pauline Chapel). His only authenticated and documented painting on panel, the Holy Family of the *Doni Tondo* (now in the Uffizi), is a powerful work, quite unlike Raphael's Madonnas, but obviously seen as competitive. Controversy and mystery surround other attributed works, which are in any case few. His drawings are numerous and often magnificent. The Sistine Ceiling is a great physical achievement apart from anything else, given the intrinsic difficulties of fresco, the area to be covered, and the awkwardness and height of the location. It took four years, with one long and other minor interruptions, so it was painted at speed, which produced both simplicity and crudeness – but then it was done to be seen from the ground, not in close-up colour photographs. Looking up at this huge mass of biblical adventures, smiling sybils and bearded prophets, one sometimes feels that it fits Dr Johnson's description of the dog walking on its hind legs: 'It is not done well; but you are surprised to find it done at all.'

Julius II's idea, when he first asked Michelangelo to paint the ceiling, was much simpler and maybe more appropriate. The painter replied that it was a 'poor' idea, meaning it did not allow him to cut a *bella figura*. So he was hoist with his own spectacular complexities. However, he completed it, in two vigorous campaigns, the second much more successful. The scheme has power, and in places noble beauty. Everyone liked it, or said they did, a mark of conventional approval that has continued to this day. (There is more dissent on whether it was finer before its recent restoration, or after.) Artists admired it, then and ever since, relieved that they themselves were spared such a horrible and difficult task, glad that a great spirit like Michelangelo took it on and made it work. It has all Michelangelo's *terribilità* and set new standards of heroic history-painting in the grand manner. As such it was an important event in European art. What more can one reasonably ask?

The *Last Judgment* is a different matter. It makes perfectly good sense as a major scheme, on a single vertical wall, like a giant canvas, with one subject. The congregation of cardinals *et al.*, attending mass, would find their eyes drifting upwards during the longueurs of the ceremony, and exploring the writhing pyramids of bodies ascending the wall or tumbling down it. The impact is frightening, as it should be. The colour is gruesome, as is also right. The great work is the apotheosis as well as the damnation of the human form, or perhaps one should say the human male form. Michelangelo worked with a determination and energy that give a forceful dynamic to the work and even a certain sinister glory. It cannot be judged from photographs and must be seen and studied and endured, no easy task in view of the jostling crowds that are there at all times. The general effect of the *Last Judgment* is to make most people think seriously about what is likely to happen to them when they die, and though they may not accept Michelangelo's version of the likely events, they are wiser for having studied it. That is exactly the effect he sought to achieve, and the work must therefore be considered successful. By comparison, the big frescoes in the Pauline Chapel, *The Conversion of St Paul* and the *Crucifixion of St Peter*, though they contain many mysteries, are routine efforts by an ageing man who no longer needed to prove himself but was anxious to justify his large stipend.

One weakness, or self-imposed limitation, emerged in all these grand projects. No one has ever devoted such attention to the human body as Michelangelo, or so little to the earth on which it is placed. He never showed any interest in locating his figures. Whilst Leonardo was fascinated by all natural phenomena, and used realism and dream-worlds for backgrounds, and whilst Raphael gives us some fascinating glimpses of early sixteenth-century Italy peering out from behind his Blessed Virgins, Michelangelo despised landscape and declined to paint it. In this restricted sense he was the quintessential Renaissance artist – art was about humanity and nothing else. But it means something is missing. On the Sistine Ceiling, God creates the sun and moon as geometrical abstractions, round lumps. In the *Last Judgment*, the blessed float up to nothing and the damned descend into a virtual vacuum. All these great decorative schemes consist of closely woven human vignettes existing in ether. It is a point of view, but not one easy for all of us to share. Dr Johnson said of Milton's *Paradise Lost*, 'No one ever wished it longer.' One might add, of Michelangelo's Sistine Chapel, 'No one ever wished it bigger.' In the end the sheer quantity of human musculature makes you wish to pass on.

But where to? Michelangelo lived on into the mid-1560s, and the Renaissance lived on with him. Had it anything more to say after his glory years? The answer must be: a great deal, and in two important respects. Michelangelo was a realist in that he drew the human shape from actual bodies with a high degree of truth to nature. But he also sought to idealize, to present human figures in their superlative ripeness, on the very verge of apotheosis. To him, the assertion that man was made in God's image was not a symbolic truism but the simple truth.

Other painters saw humanity differently and they asserted the right to contribute their own offerings to the pool of visual perception. Jacopo Pontormo (1494–1556) was a product of Andrea del Sarto's Florentine shop and was brought up to paint the ideal or the normative. But he saw people differently, or rather they had their own peculiar faces and expressions, which were normative to him. This is not so disturbing in his mythological works, which can be delightful – the fresco *Vertumnus and Pomona*, which he did around a lunette in the grand salon of the Medici villa at Poggio a Caiano, is one of the most blissful entertainments of the Renaissance, though thought-provoking on close inspection. But his sacred scenes invite comparison with the established versions and the results are worrying. In his *Visitation* (Santissima Annunziata, Florence) three holy ladies are closely grouped in swirling unity, an indelible image. The bigger group of the *Deposition* in the church of Santa Felicità in Florence is also enmeshed. It is beautiful and moving; the faces are tender and sorrowful; the colours radiant – he took the high colours of Michelangelo's

Sistine Ceiling and made them glow – but it is not natural. Pontormo's figures are not located in space. Their eyes are deep-set and often upright ovals. These figures are not real. They are creatures of Pontormo's imagination.

His fellow pupil in Andrea's shop, Rosso Fiorentino (1494–1540), showed a similar itch to get into a different world of his own. His great oil on panel, *The Deposition* (Volterra), is a fantastic composition, elegantly conceived and tenderly painted, but bears no relation to what actually happened. The setting is abstract, the faces are peculiar, though quite different to Pontormo's, the bodies are whimsical. It is Rosso's way of seeing things, his *maniera*. These languid and strange reactions to the hyperactive energy of Michelangelo and the self-confident serenity of Raphael would in a different context – say, the nineteenth century – be described as decadence. Art experts used the term Mannerism, a confusing label that no one can define.

These painters could be peculiar, Pontormo especially. He was a recluse to the point of hermitry. He built for himself an upper-room studio to which the only access was a ladder and, having stocked it up with food and water, would pull the ladder up after himself. Even his favourite pupil, Agnolo Bronzino (1503–72), was sometimes denied access, or even a response when he howled up his greetings. The pupil was more 'normal' than the master, and became the most successful painter of his generation, at least in Florence. He was court artist to the Medici dukes and painted fashionable society portraits for thirty years. His draughtsmanship was superb, his finish spectacularly lucid and transparent, the garments he put on his subjects were gorgeous but his flesh-tones were light and chilly. He froze faces in time and paint and made them peer out at us through an ice-age. The rich of his age, which coincided with the ravages of the Reformation and the early religious wars, seem stiff, inhuman, armoured, bloodless. But they liked being seen that way and now, again, we like to see them thus, so Bronzino is popular once more. Moreover, he could show a different side. His oil in the London National Gallery, *Venus, Cupid, Folly and Time*, whatever it is supposed to mean or say – argument continues among the art historians and Bronzino himself altered its scheme radically in the course of painting it –

is one of the most intriguing, erotic and lovable works to emerge during the entire Renaissance, hot blood racing through its rosy limbs and naughtiness in every inch. No wonder the Medici, anxious to suck up to France, gave it to the lustful François I!

One suspects that many painters of the *maniera* (Mannerist) period produced erotica, for which there was a rising demand at the time. Certainly Girolamo Mazzola, or Parmigianino as he is known (1503–40), did so. He made vast numbers of drawings of everyday scenes, including love-making, and many survive. His religious scenes sometimes appear frigid or, worse, frigidly sentimental, but his brilliant *Cupid*, now in Vienna, is a lubricious piece of work, calculated to appeal strongly to both sexes. Parmigianino was a prodigy who died young, and we cannot say where his alarming talents would have taken him if he had lived. Nowhere perhaps. His last major work, and his most celebrated, is a Virgin and Child attended by a group of beautiful female angels. The Child is an elongated four-footer and the Virgin's head is so far from her shoulders that this oil on panel (Uffizi) has always been known as the *Madonna of the Long Neck*.

Parmigianino came to maturity in Parma under the shadow of the great Antonio Allegri, known as Correggio after the town where he was born (1489–1534). He does not fit into a schematic presentation of the painters of the early sixteenth century because his work projects the future. We know so little about him (Vasari says he was miserly and virtuous and led a frightened life of devotion) that we cannot tell what he aimed to do. So his works have to speak for themselves. At one time he was ranked alongside Leonardo, Michelangelo, Raphael and Titian as a member of the Big Five of the Renaissance. Today his position is more precarious but rising again. He was not a Mannerist, painting real people from nature. But he was *sui generis*, an original. He did things no one had thought of doing before, either because they could not be done or were not worth doing perhaps. He painted the female nude with extraordinary skill and grace, and used his extensive interest in mythology, as was right for a man of the Renaissance, to present naked women in interesting situations. His *Io* (now in Vienna) shows an ecstatic woman in the act of being seduced by Jupiter, who appears as a furry cloud. It is painted as well as it could be, in the circumstances, but it requires a strong effort of imagination to find it erotic, which presumably was Correggio's intention. He decorated part of the Convent of San Paolo in Parma with an elaborate umbrella-vault, in which ovular glimpses of busy putti appear over semicircular classical statuettes. It is entirely original and done with ingenuity, and it gave ideas to successive generations of artists right into the eighteenth century. It was commissioned by a blue-stockinged intellectual abbess, Giovanna da Piacenza, which explains its incongruity in a house of nuns.

Later, Correggio, who was obviously conscientious and very hard-working, as well as superlatively gifted and skilled, won a prize contract to fresco the dome, apse and choir-vault of Parma Cathedral. For the dome he chose the *Assumption of the Virgin* and worked it out in immense detail, with huge supporting apostles, tiers of clouds and hundreds of swirling figures carrying the Virgin upwards. The immense work, which might have daunted even Michelangelo himself, is of course meant to be seen from beneath the dome at floor level, and Correggio used a range of illusionistic tricks and special perspectives to create his visual effects. The technical ingenuity and inventiveness is overwhelming, and the scheme made later artists marvel and seek to imitate. But it requires a willing suspension of disbelief, indeed of mirth, to get by, and one of the cathedral canons, when it was first unveiled, said it 'looked like a dish of frogs' legs'. More generally acceptable, and also widely imitated by Correggio's successors, are his lighting schemes in altarpieces and similar works, as for instance the *Adoration of the Shepherds* (Dresden), where the immensely powerful source of light appears to be the Christ-child himself. This is done with enviable skill and still leaves a strong impression, so its impact in its own time, the early 1530s, must have been prodigious. But at the top left of the painting a distinct floating cloud of heavenly bodies is awkward and incongruous (as well as unnecessary). It is a melancholy fact that Correggio's magic often teeters on the cliff-edge of the absurd and some of his finest canvases, on which he laboured so lovingly, are liable to provoke schoolboy hilarity.

No such improper ridicule is possible with Giorgione (Zorzi da

Castelfranco, 1477–1510), though his most famous painting, the oil on canvas known as *The Tempest* (Accademia, Venice), showing an almost naked beauty suckling a babe, and watched by a soldier, is peculiar, even bizarre. It was Byron's favourite painting, and it has invited endless speculation as to what it means, or is – to no effect, since the problem is now insoluble. In fact Giorgione is one of the least-documented of all the great masters, and this work is one of only four that we can be sure are his. The others are a grimly pensive portrait of a girl, *Laura* (Vienna), a wonderfully supercilious *Portrait of a Man* (San Diego) and another work in Vienna, *Boy with an Arrow*. Half a dozen other pictures are usually credited to him. They include what is perhaps the finest of all female nudes, the *Sleeping Venus* (Dresden), the *Three Philosophers* (Vienna), another mysterious work, and the delightful *Fête Champêtre* (Louvre), a joyful congress of two luscious nudes with two clothed musicians in a bosky setting, which however is also attributed to Titian, or both. Giorgione died suddenly of the plague, aged thirty-three, and his work in progress was finished by Titian or by Sebastiano del Piombo, who probably worked in his shop.

The fact that we know so little about Giorgione, and that, of the sixty-six works once attributed to him, only a handful survive modern critical scrutiny, make it difficult to evaluate his contribution to the history of art. But he was clearly important, for various early authorities call him the founder of the 'modern' (that is, post-Bellini) Venetian school. His unusual range of subject-matter, his originality, his fine sense of colour, the striking way in which he composed a picture, his rendering of human, especially female, flesh, so totally different to the muscularity of his contemporary Michelangelo, all these qualities – and others – mark him out as a pioneer. He seems to have worked under Giovanni Bellini, as did his partner, Vincenzo Catena (1475–1531), and Bellini gave him the passion for landscape that infuses *The Tempest*, and almost dominates *The Three Philosophers*, so that the trees and rocks, painted from nature with wondrous skill, are an integral part of the composition. Even when Giorgione takes on a straightforward subject, he creates enigmas. His altarpiece in Castelfranco, done in tempera on panel, is of the *Virgin Enthroned with St George and St Francis*. Why is she thrust onto an enormous stone and wooden edifice, twenty feet high, so that she is pushed to the top rear of the picture, leaving the two saints to dominate the foreground which is set on an alfresco marble floor? The lady and her attendant landscape, rendered beautifully, are almost a separate picture. And there is a sinister male figure in the background, casting a huge shadow. But there is no end to the puzzles that this painter sets. He fills us with delightful speculation.

Without Giorgione, certainly, there could have been no Titian (Tiziano Vecellio, c. 1485–1576) as we have him. He built industriously on his Venetian heritage, worked hard all his long life, performed well in all its various departments – history, sacred art, portraits, mythology and allegory – and came to dominate not only Italian but European painting in the mid-sixteenth century. Working not only for the leading Italian patrons (from his base in Venice) but for such world figures as the Emperor Charles V and his son Philip II of Spain, he was the first master to bind European art together and enable us to consider it as a whole. Indeed, his work, especially in its earlier stages, was a compendium of Italian Renaissance art as it existed at the end of the first quarter of the sixteenth century.

This epitomizing spirit is beautifully illustrated in his great painting in London's National Gallery, *Bacchus and Ariadne*. It was one of three that Titian created for Alfonso d'Este, Duke of Ferrara, for a *camerino* (small room) in his castle there. The duke had wanted the room to contain work from all the leading painters of the day, but for one reason or another Raphael, Fra Bartolommeo and Michelangelo did not contribute, and Titian incorporated their ideas in the three paintings (oil on canvas) that he supplied, as well as what he had learned from Giorgione. The *Bacchus* is an amazingly vivid and accomplished work: vigorous figures and plenty of action, an enchanting child faun, dogs and leopards and a snake, rich colours for vestments, magnificent trees, a subtly painted landscape, a dazzling sky that was to become an overworked cliché in the hands of later practitioners, such as Poussin, but was then new and fresh – the whole worked cunningly into a composition of magical variety, balance and unity. This was the

Renaissance at its opulent maturity, serene and self-assured, fascinating in detail, powerful in its central thrust. It and similar works became the standard against which the best painters measured themselves for two centuries.

Titian also laid down the parameters within which portraiture would be conducted. He moved from the typical Renaissance head and shoulders (often in profile) to the half-length, three-quarter and even full-length. He painted the face from all angles. He got the most out of the richest possible draperies and garments, in strong, warm colours. He painted the Emperor Charles V on his warhorse, with huge success, thus setting another fashion that lasted until the age of Bonaparte. He painted Pope Paul III, conveying shiftiness, piety and austerity. He painted scores of beautiful women, clothed and unclothed, dwelling on their voluptuousness, sensuality and occasionally their intelligence. His portraits filled the rich, the powerful and the famous with awe and made them queue to sit to him, and drove other painters back to their studios itching to use the brush in emulation.

The brushwork was the key, because although Titian drew well in his youth, few drawings survive from later periods. He worked directly on the canvas, with only slight underdrawing, and often with no preliminary sketches at all. This was contrary to all the best practice, in the view of the Florentines, who thought that a work should be composed in line and underlay, then completed by applying paint on top of the already existing tonal structure. But Titian might well have argued that the real world is composed not of lines but of forms and that colour is part of the forms, intrinsic to them. He built up the forms with colour, not lines. It allowed for spontaneity, abrupt changes of mind or atmosphere; it unleashed the genius of a master-painter. In a way, it was as great a change as the use of oil paint itself. It is the method most painters have followed ever since. But it is open to abuse, and as he became an old man, Titian abused it. He stopped using underdrawing at all and laid down layers of paint on which to build his structures. His brushstrokes became thicker and cruder, and he used his fingers as well as his brushes. Sometimes the effects he thus achieved were sensational, but more often they make you long to get back to the time of Giorgione.

The golden age of Venetian Renaissance painting was brought to an end, and the work of Titian complemented by a coda in the shape of Jacopo Robusti or Tintoretto (1519–94). He came from a family of local painters, worked in the city virtually all his life, adorned many of its chief public buildings, including the Doge's Palace, and covered vast areas of canvas. His output was huge: there are, for instance, at least eight *Last Suppers* by him, some on a monumental scale. He carried Titian's methods of painting still further and developed what is known as the *prestezza* technique of rapid brushstrokes, creating impressions of faces and objects rather than working them out in detail. His major paintings are designed to be seen from a distance rather than minutely inspected from close up. But of course most people, especially patrons, want both: they survey from afar, then move in to inspect the workmanship. Many of them in sixteenth-century Venice considered Tintoretto's work unfinished. They wanted him to have another go, and he refused. They turned instead to an artist from Verona, Paolo Caliari, known as Veronese (1528–88), who painted on an equally large scale but produced a more finished and smooth effect, and introduced the sumptuous settings and luxurious garments that Venetian high society loved.

Hence Tintoretto ended his life a comparatively poor man, and his widow had to petition the authorities for help. At his best, however, he achieved tremendous effects, of a kind Titian never even attempted. In his parish church of Santa Maria del Orto, where he is buried, he created a cataclysmic *Last Judgment*, which in many ways is more impressive than Michelangelo's in the Sistine Chapel. It is the end of the world presented in the most dramatic fashion, and a fit point at which to bring this survey to a close. Within a few years, Caravaggio had introduced his new and spectacular epoch of realism, and scattered the last, lingering leaves of the Renaissance to the four winds.

PART SIX

The Spread and Decline of the Renaissance

The spread of Renaissance ideas and forms within Italy was, initially, slow, and outside Italy it was slower still. To northern minds and eyes, what we (not they; they had no name for it, it was normality) call Gothic was immensely satisfying and therefore tenacious. The fourteenth and fifteenth centuries saw a gracious flowering in painting, sculpture and architecture in parts of northern Europe, especially in Burgundy and the Low Countries, France and southern Germany. It culminated in the great panels of Jan van Eyck, in the magnificent illustrations by the Limburg brothers to the *Très Riches Heures du Duc de Berry*, and in lofty cathedrals and splendid châteaux. In England, the latest phase of its insular style of late Gothic, Perpendicular, was still absolutely dominant in the first quarter of the sixteenth century. It was one of the most creative periods in European history, but what was done was in 'the old style'; it was the art of the Middle Ages, refined, improved, more ornate and elaborate, but still medieval. Northern scholars were already avidly reading recovered Greek and Roman texts but artists did not yet look to antiquity for models.

The first northerner to apply himself seriously to what was going on in the arts in Italy was Albrecht Dürer (1471–1528), the painter son of a Nuremberg goldsmith. An engraver himself, he caught glimpses of Italian ideas through prints, and in 1494, aged twenty-three, he went to Venice himself. He progressed slowly south on foot, punctuating his journey by a series of delightful watercolours, recording his amazement at the light and colour of the South, the olive groves and the strange architecture (his view of Arco, painted on his return journey, is the first European landscape masterpiece done in watercolour). He learned a great deal in Italy, and he returned again in 1505–7 to learn more. Later in life he set down his impressions, in theoretical writings, especially his *Treatise on Measurement*. Germany, he said, was full of budding painters, 'able boys', who were simply dumped on a master and told to copy him. 'They were taught without any rational principle and solely according to the old usage. And thus they grew up in ignorance, like a wild and unpruned tree.' In Italy, he said, he learned the importance of mathematics in art: the need to measure every part of the human body to get accuracy, the need to apply oneself to perspective scientifically, so that properly drawn bodies could be placed realistically in space. Dürer added that he learned from the writings of Pliny that the masters of the antique age – Apelles, Protogenes, Phidias, Praxiteles and others – had studied the crafts of painting and sculpture systematically and with science, and had even written books about their skills. But these had been lost, and so had what he called 'the rational foundations of art'. Hence 'art was extinct until it came to light again [in Italy] one century and a half ago.' Dürer, a modest but determined man, said he aimed to show people outside Italy how art ought to be conducted, however limited his own skills and knowledge, and he invited critics to point out 'the errors of my present work' so that 'even so, I shall have been the cause of the truth coming to light'. We see in Dürer a man who had acquired the true Renaissance perspective: the rejection of medieval art as false; the need to examine the work of antiquity both in practice, by studying its survivals, and in theory, by reading the texts; the concentration on the human form, and its exact representation by scientific study; and the mastering of perspective.

It is important to emphasize what Dürer actually said about the influence of Italian standards on northern art, for recent historical scholarship has tended to suggest that artistic interaction north and south of the Alps constituted a two-way process, rather than a simple acquisition of Italian ideas by still-medieval northerners. This was the message of the important Lorenzo Lotto exhibition at the National Gallery, Washington, in 1997; the display of Renaissance art in the Netherlands at the Metropolitan Museum, New York, in 1998; and the exhibition, 'Renaissance Venice and the North', held at the Palazzo Grassi in 1999–2000. The weighty catalogues that accompanied these exhibitions presented the evidence of a northern contribution to Italian Renaissance art in considerable detail. But Dürer was a practising artist, alive and travelling on both sides of the Alps at the time, not an academic writing half a millennium later, and he was quite clear about the relationship between north and south in art. For him, a German painter, a visit to Italy was an artistic revelation, what we would call a culture-shock.

Dürer was unusually thoughtful and articulate for a painter, and in effect tells us how the Italian Renaissance changed him; we can trace the consequences in his work. But in this as in other respects, he was unique. His contemporary, Mathias Grünewald (c. 1470–1528), gives us no hint of the way in which the new perspective ideas, and the rendering of the human form 'by science', influenced his Isenheim altarpiece (1515), as they clearly did. Albrecht Altdorfer (c. 1480–1538) made splendid and highly individualistic use of the Italian revival of classical mythology but was silent about his aims. But sometimes a work of art itself speaks. In 1506, while Dürer was on his second visit to Italy, Lucas Cranach the elder (1472–1553) was painting an altar-triptych, *The Martyrdom of St Catherine*, using oils on limewood, which is now in Dresden. Catherine, one of the most popular saints among medieval artists, was a high-born lady of fourth-century Alexandria. She declined a marriage proposal from the emperor Maxentius, successfully disputed with fifty pagan philosophers on the merits of Christianity, and was condemned to be broken on the wheel. But it was the wheel that was broken by a divine thunderbolt and many of the pagans were roasted with it. In the end they had to behead the brave lady.

Cranach treats this fantastic story with a mesmeric *mélange* of realism and extravagance. The scene is set under a threatening German sky, lit by lightning. Wittenberg, shown in brilliant detail, is in the top left-hand corner of the central panel, and Cranach portrays the elite of the city – professors, theologians and nobility – among the crowd surrounding Catherine, who are being converted by her pious eloquence. The great humanist Schwarzenberg falls from his horse. Frederick the Wise looks puzzled. Friends and patrons, lovingly depicted, are swept into the catastrophe, their souls saved, their bodies about to be destroyed. The colours are light, fresh, dazzling. Flowers, trees, ferns and exotic grasses abound. In the midst of it all, Catherine, beautiful and undismayed, kneels serene, awaiting her death and sanctification with confidence. She is dressed in her best clothes, as a bride of Christ: a superb gown of scarlet velvet with heavy gold trimmings, exquisite Brussels lace on her wrists, rubies and pearls hanging on her breast, with a gold collar round her shoulders. Her red hair is carefully curled. Her executioner, in the art of drawing his sword, is just as elegant. His handsome blond face is that of Pfeffinger, the king's counsellor. He is tall, slim, riotously dressed in the latest fashion, with striped hose in black, red and white, gold silk ribbons tied just below the knees, and a slashed gold silk jacket embroidered with flowers. His page is equally chic, and in one of the side-panels, an enchanting boy, modelled on John Frederick, the king's son, distributes flowers to three beautiful saints, St Dorothy, St Agnes and St Kunigund, having already decorated himself with a coronet of blossoms. Three equally luscious ladies, St Barbara, St Ursula and St Margaret, stand in the other side-panel, accompanied by a domesticated dragon and under the protection of Coburg Castle. This wonderful work, Cranach's masterpiece, breathes joy and godliness, despite its sensational subject. It is an incongruous but somehow deeply satisfying mixture of medieval, northern values with the thrilling new spirit from the South, a hymn of happiness to the German discovery of the Renaissance. But, produced as it was, at the beginning of the High Renaissance in Rome, it would have had Italian sophisticates roaring with laughter. It was the kind of painting that Michelangelo dismissed as 'external accuracy [but] done without reason or true art, without symmetry or proportion', a view that was reflected a generation or so later in Vasari's *Lives of the Painters*.

And if the northerners, Dürer excepted, were largely silent about the spread of the Renaissance, so also were those Italians who carried it north of the Alps. Pietro Torrigiano (1475–1528), the Florentine sculptor, came to England to create, for Henry VIII, the tomb-images of his father and mother in Westminster Abbey in 1511–18, but left no record of his visit. We know (from Vasari) that he broke Michelangelo's nose in a brawl but not how he brought Renaissance sculpture to London. Leonardo's life in France is fairly well documented but he did not describe how he carried the Renaissance with him; nor did Rosso Fiorentino or

Francesco Primaticcio when they decorated the great gallery at Fontainebleau for François I.

Printing and gunpowder did the work, in all probability, more effectively than anything else. We have already noted the extra-ordinarily rapid spread of printing in Europe. And printing brought with it comparatively cheap engravings, which disseminated Italian notions of the human form and perspective, and the delights of classical mythology, throughout European society, and especially in the workshops of craftsmen and artists. From the early years of the sixteenth century, Renaissance visual tech-niques and patterns are to be found in pottery and silverware, in elaborate goldsmiths' work, in tapestry, silks, rich cloths, even in furniture, all over Europe.

Gunpowder encouraged campaigning over long distances, and in the wake of armies came curious princes eager to collect. The French were in Italy from the mid-1490s, ravaging and looting but also learning and acquiring. They were followed by the imperial Germans, who marched up and down the peninsula, knocking over duchies and principalities, but also keeping their eyes open for the new. States were growing more powerful, with access to more money to spend on self-glorification, so architecture, as the most visible of the arts to all, led the way in using Italian Renaissance forms and decorative features to enhance the splen-dour of foreign princes. Between the 1490s and the 1550s, the French crown grew rapidly in strength, and flexed its muscles not only in war but in building. François I was one of the most extravagant builders of all time, and along the banks of the Loire he imported Renaissance ideas in profusion and transformed them into French castle-palaces of great size and elaboration. Chambord in particular became one of the most remarkable buildings in Europe. These palaces had to be adorned and filled with beauty. So in the wake of the builders came the decorators and painters, the furniture-makers and *tapissiers*.

The rise of the Habsburgs was also a prime factor in the spread of the Renaissance. Charles V, ruler of Austria and the Netherlands, Emperor of Germany and King of Spain and its dependencies, was something approaching a world ruler, and an art patron on a magnificent scale. To him, art had no frontiers, Europe was a cultural unity, and artists of all kinds were recruited wherever they lived, and sped at his bidding. In the heart of the old Moorish palace of Granada, acquired by Spain in 1492 when the Moors were expelled, he set the stamp of the Italian Renaissance by erecting an incongruous classical building, a columned circle within a square, to show he was master. And, later, in the Palace of the Escorial outside Madrid, he created an enormous complex in which ideas imported from Renaissance Italy were transmuted into dramatic Spanish forms.

Italian ideas penetrated central and eastern Europe, in some cases well before the sixteenth century. It was in Hungary, for instance, that buildings in the style of the Renaissance made their first appearance outside Italy. King Matthias Corvinus of Hungary (1458–90) was a warrior and conqueror and an enthusiast for the antique. He looked back to the Roman Empire for inspiration and to Italians to serve him in recreating some of its aspects. In 1467 he imported Rodolfo Fioravanti, known as 'Aristotle', who had worked on the Vatican obelisk with Alberti and was 'skilled in moving heavy objects'. He was an engineer and a military architect and he built a bridge in Buda, the Hungarian capital. Corvinus got Pollaiuolo to design the drapes for his throne room, Caradosso to produce gold altarpieces for the cathedral at Esztergom, and Filippo Lippi to supply two beautiful panels, according to Vasari. Many Italian artist-craftsmen were active in Hungary in the years after Corvinus's death. Thus the Bakocz Chapel at Esztergom Cathedral (built from 1506) is one of the most dazzling examples of High Renaissance architecture outside Italy.

The expatriate Italian artists, who were immensely adaptable, proved able to work successfully in alien vernaculars, adapting them to Renaissance models. Thus Fioravanti went on from Buda to Russia in 1474, and began work on the Dormition Cathedral inside the Kremlin. Earlier efforts by local craftsmen to erect this building had failed. Fioravanti produced a mason's level, a compass and drawing tools, and by superior science, as well as art – he used brick and cement instead of sand and gravel for wall-filling, as well as modern stonecutting techniques and hoisting machines – he had completed the building by 1479. A generation later, another Italian, Alessio Novi, built the church of St Michael-Archangel, also within the Kremlin walls (1505–9). The Jagellonian dynasty of Poland likewise imported Italians, and had local artists trained in the Renaissance manner. Thus in the cathedral of Wawel Castle in Cracow, the splendid Renaissance tomb of Jan Olbracht (1502–5) is the joint work of Francesco Fiorentino and Stanislas Stoss, and the grand courtyard of the castle, built a little later, is also by Francesco working with a local 'Master Benedikt'. These are only some of many examples of the early penetration by the Renaissance of eastern-central Europe collected in a recent study.[1]

By the end of the 1520s, of course, Renaissance ideas and forms of art were being recreated or adapted in most parts of Europe and even in the New World. Titian, coming to the height of his powers, was not just an Italian but a European artist. As we have seen, by 1500 literary humanism was a pan-European movement, and where humanist books penetrated, Renaissance art was sure to follow soon. However, by this date in history, the Renaissance was being affected not only by its own internal modulations but by external events. In the fourteenth and fifteenth centuries, Italy had not exactly been tranquil – on the contrary, there had been periodic and often highly destructive fighting between the leading cities for local and regional hegemony – but there had been comparatively little interference from abroad. It was during this period of Italian independence that urban life flourished and prospered and the Renaissance took hold. However, in September 1494, Charles VIII of France, at the invitation of the Duke of Milan, entered Italy with an army to conquer the Kingdom of Naples, and brought Italy's political isolation to an end. Thereafter, Italy was rent by two ravenous foreign dogs, Valois France and Habsburg Germany, until the Peace of Cateau-Cambrensis of 1558. The fighting was periodic rather than continuous and it did not affect the whole of Italy. But it was on a scale the country had never known before, involving massive use of cannon and the consequent need to build expensive walls and forts round the towns.

Charles VIII's expedition had an immediate effect on Florence, for it led to the flight of the Medici, the 'liberation' of Pisa from Florence by Charles, and his triumphant entry into Florence itself. He did not stay long, hurrying on to Naples and failure, but his inruption introduced a period of turmoil which produced the iconoclastic mission of Savonarola and his unseemly trial and incineration. Florence continued to produce great art and artists but it was 'never glad confident morning again'. From the perspective of history, we can now see that the Florentine Renaissance came to a climax in the quarter-century before the French invasion, when it truly was a city made for artists.[2]

The centre of artistic activity then shifted to Rome, under a series of munificent popes, especially Julius II and his Medici successor Leo X. This was the great Roman age of Raphael and Michelangelo. But the French kings continued their forays into Italy, and rising Spanish–German power found a champion in the young Emperor Charles V. François I was decisively defeated, and taken prisoner, at the Battle of Pavia in 1525, making the Germans masters of Italy, and two years later Charles's army of mercenaries, somewhat against his wishes, entered and sacked Rome. That, it could be said, ended the High Renaissance, and the Roman cultural climate was not the same again for half a century. Wars, rumours of wars and even occupations of cities did not necessarily bring artistic activity to an end. Indeed, it is remarkable how often artists were able to carry on, discharging important commissions, during periods of turmoil. But the loss of Italian self-respect that the constant foreign invasions produced, and the periodic impoverishment of large parts of the countryside, had their inevitable consequences. It is not surprising, therefore, that after the sack of Rome artistic leadership in Italy tended to go to Venice which, though involved in the various coalitions that invasion forced the cities to put together, was itself spared direct attack. But the truth is, by the mid-century, the absolute predominance that Italy had once exercised in the arts was passing, as France, Germany, the Netherlands, Spain and even England began to acquire cultural self-confidence. Thus at the time when the ideas of the Italian Renaissance were spreading with increasing speed all over Europe, the source itself was burning low.

There was the growing religious factor too. Medieval Europe was in some ways a totalitarian society, in that the Catholic Church permitted no competitors in giving intellectual and spiritual guidance, employing the civic power to suppress heresy by force. In theory it sought to control every aspect of cultural activity. In practice it was often surprisingly liberal or comatose, and artists went on with their own visual and decorative schemes unsupervised. Nudity was not on the whole permitted by public opinion, but an enormous spread of Christian mythology and miraculous happenings, much of it mere folklore without a biblical sanction at all, grew from its roots in popular credulity to provide artists with wondrous subject-matter. Towards the close of the Middle Ages, these fantastic and magical tales were intertwined with symbolism and allegory to produce strange visions, as in the works of Hieronymus Bosch (c. 1450–1516), though it is well to realize that Bosch's appeal to his contemporaries was not the same as to us: Henry III of Nassau bought his *Garden of Earthly Delights* not so much because he thought it edifying but because he and his guests found it 'curious' and funny.[3]

The painters of the Renaissance benefited greatly from this freedom or laxity. They were of course subject to the detailed directions or whims of their ecclesiastical patrons, who were often pernickety, as many surviving contracts testify. But there was no central control, telling artists what to do or what not to do. The popes themselves were sometimes humanists, as witness Pius II (pope 1458–64), or were generally sympathetic to the aims of the Renaissance. That was true of all the popes from Sixtus IV, elected in 1471, to Clement VII, elected in 1523. Bearing in mind that the Renaissance was in one important respect a celebration of the artistic and intellectual virtues of pagan antiquity, and their application to modern civilized life, the degree of tolerance was remarkable. That the head of the Roman Catholic Church should not only permit, but commission and pay for scenes of pagan mythology was taken for granted as a rule, and only a few hardy spirits, like Savonarola, questioned it. His fate can therefore be seen as a victory for Renaissance values, though it is doubtful if Botticelli saw it that way.

However, the broad-mindedness of the church was a feature of its absolute unity and supremacy. When these disappeared or were challenged, a different spirit began to emerge, on both sides of the religious divide. The origins of the Reformation, which began to have an impact on events in the 1520s, were complex, but the Renaissance clearly played its part. Among the humanists, the spirit of criticism was the most marked characteristic. In their search for the recovery of an ideal past, they looked hard at everything in the present. They not only identified faulty texts and spurious documents, they also turned a critical eye on institutions and practices. And from the point of view of the intellectuals, the most important institution by far was the church and its controlling machinery in Rome. On Rome, and what it permitted, they focussed more and more. Just as they delighted to strip an ancient text of its medieval accretions, so they sought to reduce the proliferating practices of the church, which had become nauseous to many educated people, to find the primitive, apostolic and pentecostal church beneath. So the reform movement in the church was broadly similar to the Renaissance itself in its aims and methods, and it is in this sense that Erasmus, greatest of the humanists, was later said to have 'laid the egg of the Reformation'.

Since the Reformation was about the removal of medieval accretions to the integrity of primitive Christianity, which included of course the power of the papacy, it was inevitable that the aims of the humanists and those of the Reformers should become confused. The humanists were concerned not only about the way Latin was written, aiming to replace the medieval demotic by classic purity, but about its pronunciation. They were particularly anxious to show how Greek should be promoted, dismissing the clerical usage as barbarous. By the 1530s in England, for instance, Reformers, or 'heretics', were often identified in the minds of suspicious conservative churchmen by the 'newfangled' way they spoke Greek. Music became another source of cultural-religious contention. There had long been grumbles within the church about the way in which polyphony and other proliferating musical devices were obscuring the meaning of the words sung in masses and other sacred music. In 1324 the Avignon pope John XXII issued a bad-tempered decree condemning 'certain disciples of the new school' for 'preferring to devise ways of their own rather than to continue singing in the old manner'. He complained that 'the divine office is now performed with semibreves and minims, and with these notes of small value every composition is pestered. Moreover, they truncate the melodies with hockets, they deprave them with discantus' and so on, in an exasperated tone – ending lamely, however, that disobedience would be punished by 'suspension from office of eight days'.

Little notice was taken of this warning, or of others, and sacred music continued to become more complicated and, to the layman, incomprehensible. This, it should be said, was typical Gothic multiplication of complexity, the exact counterpart of the fantastically ornate architecture – late Perpendicular, Plateresque, etc – that was prevalent in the second half of the fourteenth and fifteenth centuries. It had nothing to do with Renaissance antiquarianism. It is not clear whether there was such a phenomenon as Renaissance music, as opposed to music during the Renaissance. The 'new art', as it was called, of musical notation had been introduced around 1316 by a Frenchman, Philippe de Vitry (1291–1361). This made notation far more flexible and allowed composers to express their wishes with clarity and to introduce far more varieties of rhythm. Certainly Italian musicians played only a minor part in musical development in the closing centuries of the Middle Ages. Changes came from France, the Low Countries and England. It is notable that, whereas in the visual arts Italy exported innovators and masters, in music it imported them. The most celebrated musical composer and organizer of the entire period, Adrian Willaerts (c. 1490–1562), came from Bruges. After holding various posts in Italy he was appointed in 1527 *maestro di capella* at St Mark's, Venice, at a salary that eventually rose to the enormous sum of 200 ducats a year. Apart from composing nine masses and innumerable other works, sacred and secular, he made the music at St Mark's the best in Europe, rivalled only by companies run by the emperor, the kings of England and France, the Pope and the courts of Mantua and Ferrara.

Italy, then, at least had the credit of maintaining four out of the seven best musical ensembles in Europe. It also played a role in the technology of music, including the development of the lute, the violin, the viol, the trumpet and woodwind, and such keyboard instruments as the harpsichord and the virginal. By the late sixteenth century, compositions required instruments with four octaves and the whole chromatic range. Venice was the first printing centre to start (1501) reproducing scores, and these sixteenth-century print-runs were often extensive, 500 to 2000 copies. Moreover, in music as well as the other arts, Italy led the way in resuscitating antiquity, publishing Isadore of Seville (1470) as well as the musical writings of Plato and Aristotle. During the first quarter of the sixteenth century, translations of the treatises on music by Ptolemy and Baccheus were in print and by 1562 so was the first translation of Aristoxenus' *Harmonics*. In 1581 Vincenzo Galilei, in his *Dialogo della musica antica e della moderna*, actually reproduced three ancient Greek hymns by Mesomedes, which had come down through Byzantium.[4]

There is evidence that, in the sixteenth century, knowledge of music was spreading in the towns of Europe, and that a bourgeois market was opening to supplement the princely one. But the Reformers insisted that religion had to be popular, which meant it should be presented in the vernacular – itself a Renaissance notion – and that meant all the old settings in Latin had to be discarded. Moreover, the more rigorous Reformers insisted, rather on the lines of John XXII, that complexity of setting was inadmissible, and in particular that no more than one note should be sung on each syllable, or even each word, so that congregations could follow the text. Rejecting the mass, with its complex settings, they favoured church music that was simple and biblical, such as psalmody, producing straightforward metrical settings of the psalms that could be roared out by vast congregations (e.g., at the services held at the cross outside St Paul's Cathedral in London). The Reformers, led by Luther himself, also wrote vernacular hymns, with a strong biblical content, set to non-polyphonic music.

Such developments, as well as the general use of the vernacular in church services, proved popular, especially in the towns, where more and more citizens were becoming literate and read the Bible for themselves. By the 1540s, the Catholic Church was not only losing northern Germany, much of France, England, Scotland and Scandinavia, but was finding itself on the cultural defensive everywhere. It reacted in a number of different ways, which were often inconsistent. First, it increased the activities of the Inquisition, especially in Spain (where it was run essentially by the state) and in Italy (where it was run by the papacy). Second, it created new orders, such as the Jesuits, whose chief thrust was in education at all levels. Third, it became more puritanical. The papacy in particular ceased to patronize artists who favoured papal mythology and the nude, and covered up the private parts of male statues. Fourth, it began to reform itself. This took many forms, but the most important were the proper training of priests, the creation of seminaries and colleges, and the activities of key members of the episcopate, such as the great St Charles Borromeo, the Cardinal-Archbishop of Milan. Reform took on an institutional aspect when the Council of Trent was summoned in 1545. It sat for most of two decades, with intermissions, and only in its concluding stages did it turn directly to cultural matters.

By this point, the Catholic Church had been identified with the 'old' music, that is, any music with Latin texts and polyphonic content. Most professional musicians, even in predominantly Protestant societies, were Catholics: their livelihood was at stake. Queen Elizabeth of England, though Protestant, had an all-Catholic Chapel Royal, which was the target of attack by the advanced Reformers, particularly those with Puritan leanings. By protecting the Catholic performers and composers, she saved English music. But polyphony, and everything associated with it, was under attack within the Catholic Church, even in Rome itself. In 1549, one Italian bishop, Cirillo Franco, said of polyphonic masses: 'When one voice says *Sanctus*, another says *Sabbaoth*, so that they sound more like cats in January than flowers in May.' Ten years before, Giovanni Morone, Bishop of Modena, had actually abolished polyphony in his own cathedral in favour of plainchant, and he was one of the papal legates supervising the discussion of church music when the Council of Trent finally got round to it in 1562-3. There is a famous story, or legend, that the master of music at Santa Maria Maggiore in Rome, the composer Giovanni Palestrina (1525-94), produced his *Missa Papae Marcelli*, for a special performance, to show that polyphony could be combined with intelligibility, and that this had the desired effect. Whether the story is true or not, it is a fact that Trent ended without any destructive ruling on music.

It was a different matter with painting. Here the Council in its final session ruled that stories about sacred personages that were not to be found in the canonical texts, and saintly miracles that the church had not certified as probable, were not to figure in works of art to be placed in churches or other religious buildings. It was not, strictly speaking, an act of iconoclasm, since it was prospective, not retrospective. Few existing images were removed, as had already been done in countless buildings controlled by Protestant zealots. But it put a stop to any future work of that kind and thus robbed religious artists of one of their chief sources of subject-matter. It was the end of the Middle Ages, abolishing at a stroke the swarming inventiveness and labyrinthine imagination that had produced so much delightful art, both in the Gothic mode and indeed in Renaissance works, where Christian and pagan mythology intertwined. It affected not only the great masters working in the big cities, but also – and perhaps more – the humble artist-craftsmen of the smaller towns and villages, whose wall-paintings, bench ends and shrine figures had been encyclopaedias of Christian folklore, now all forbidden.

Even more influential were the more positive doctrines of the Counter-Reformation, which the final session of Trent formalized. In response to the Protestant cult of the vernacular – of simplicity, austerity and puritanism – the Catholic Church, after its earlier defensive and guilt-ridden response, decided to embark on a much bolder policy of emphasizing the spectacular. With the Jesuits in the vanguard, churches and other religious buildings were to be ablaze with light, clouded with incense, draped in lace, smothered in gilt, with huge altars, splendid vestments, sonorous organs and vast choirs, and a liturgy purged of medieval nonsense but essentially triumphalist in its content and amplitude. The artists – painters, sculptors, architects, makers of church furniture and windows – were to fall into line, scrapping the folklore and mythology indeed, but portraying the story of Christianity, the history of the church, the faith of its martyrs and the destruction of its enemies with all the power and realism they could command. Thus Rome defied the Protestants and bid the Puritans do their worst. Catholicism would reply to simplicity and primitive austerity with all the riches and colour and swirling lines and glitter in its repertory, adding new ones as artists could create them.

Whatever the spiritual merits of this policy, it was undoubtedly popular in southern Europe at least, and in the closing decades of the sixteenth century the Catholic Church began to regain some lost ground. However, the Counter-Reformation approach to art was a formula for what would later be called the Baroque. It was music in the ears of ambitious young painters like Caravaggio. But it tolled a requiem for the Renaissance, or rather the attitudes it stood for. The movement was already a spent force anyway, and by the 1560s and 1570s it was dead, as dead as Michelangelo and Titian, its last great masters. But Renaissance forms lingered on. They had become part of the basic repertoire of European arts, subsumed in the Baroque and in Rococo, ready to spring to life again in the neoclassicism of the late eighteenth century. They are with us still. In many ways the ideals of those times are part of our permanent cultural heritage, as are the matchless works of art and the enduring monuments those rich and fruitful times produced.

Notes

1. *Court, Cloister and City: the Art and Culture of Central Europe, 1450–1800* by Thomas DaCosta Kaufmann (London, 1995), Chapter One.
2. See *Renaissance Florence: the Art of the 1470s* by Patricia Lee Rubin and Alison Wright (London, 1999).
3. See *Gombrich on the Renaissance*, vol. 3 (London, 1993), pp. 79ff.
4. For Renaissance music see *The New Grove Dictionary of Music*, vol. 15; and *Music in the Age of the Renaissance* by L. L. Perkins (New York, 1999).

Bibliography

The literature on every aspect of the Renaissance is endless, and
I confine myself here to books in my own library which I have
consulted for this work. First and foremost the *Grove Dictionary
of Art*, edited by Jane Turner (34 vols., London, 1996), especially
for dates, spelling of proper names and whereabouts of paintings
and sculptures. It is particularly valuable for its bibliographies. I
have also used the *New Grove Dictionary of Music*, edited by
Stanley Sadie (20 vols., London, 1995), for fifteenth- and sixteenth-
century music. Older general books include J. Burckhardt, *The
Civilisation of the Renaissance in Italy* (first published in
Germany in 1860) and Bernard Berenson, *Italian Painters of the
Renaissance* (Oxford, 1953). The works of Kenneth Clark are
also still valuable, especially his essays collected in *The Art of
Humanism* (London, 1983), his *Leonardo da Vinci* (revised edition,
London, 1989), and his *Leonardo Drawings at Windsor Castle* (2
vols., Cambridge, 1935). E. H. Gombrich's essays are collected in
Gombrich on the Renaissance (3 vols., London, 1993). I also used
C. F. Black *et al.*, *Cultural Atlas of the Renaissance* (New York,
1993); the Einaudi *History of Italian Art* (2 vols., in translation,
Cambridge, 1994); Denis Hay, *The Italian Renaissance in its
Historical Background* (Cambridge, 1979); John White, *Art and
Architecture in Italy, 1250–1400* (New Haven, 1993); J. Shearman,
Early Italian Pictures in the Royal Collection (Cambridge, 1983);
M. Levey, *Later Italian Pictures in the Royal Collection*
(Cambridge, 1991); E. Welch, *Art and Society in Italy, 1350–
1500* (Oxford, 1997); M. Davies and D. Gordon, *The Early Italian
Schools before 1400* (London, 1998); S. J. Freedberg, *Painting in
Italy 1500–1600* (London, 1993); N. Huse and W. Wolters, *Art of
Renaissance Venice* (New York, 1993); A. Chastel, *History of
French Art; the Renaissance* (2 vols., in translation, London, 1973);
J. Dunkerton *et al.*, *Giotto to Dürer: Early Renaissance Painting*

in the National Gallery (London, 1991); various writings by John Pope-Hennessy, *Italian High Renaissance and Baroque Sculpture* (ed., London, 1996), *Essays on Italian Sculpture* (London, 1968), *Italian Gothic Sculpture* (London, 1955), and *The Portrait in the Renaissance* (Oxford, 1966). Also, E. Panofsky, *Renaissance and Renaissances in Western Art* (2 vols., Stockholm, 1960).

More detailed studies include: A. J. Lemaître and E. Lessing, *Florence and the Renaissance: the Quattrocento* (Paris, 1993); G. Brucker, *Florence: the Golden Age* (Berkeley, 1998); P. L. Rubin and A. Wright, *Renaissance Florence: the Art of the 1470s* (London, 1999); A. Paolucci, *The Origins of Renaissance Art: the Baptistry Doors, Florence* (in translation, New York, 1996); D. Norman (ed.), *Siena, Florence and Padua: Art, Society and Religion 1280–1400* (2 vols., London, 1995); A. M. Romanini, *Assisi: the Frescoes in the Basilica of St Francis* (New York, 1999); John White, *The Birth and Rebirth of Pictorial Space* (London, 1967); S. J. Freedberg, *Painting of the High Renaissance in Rome and Florence* (2 vols., revised edition, New York, 1989); and Emile Mâle, *Religious Art in France: the Late Middle Ages* (in translation, Princeton, 1986).

Studies of individuals and specific works of art include: B. A. Bennett and D. G. Wilkins, *Donatello* (Oxford, 1984); James Beck, *Jacopo della Quercia* (2 vols., New York, 1991); John Pope-Hennessy, *Cellini* (New York, 1985); C. Avery and D. Finn, *Giambologna* (Oxford, 1987); Howard Saalman, *Filippo Brunelleschi: the Buildings* (London, 1993); D. Howard, *Jacopo Sansovino: Architecture and Patronage in Renaissance Venice* (London, 1987); G. Kreytenberg, *Orcagna's Tabernacle in Or San Michele, Florence* (New York, 1994); Colin Eisler, *Jacopo Bellini: Complete Paintings and Drawings* (New York, 1989); S. Fermor, *Piero di Cosimo* (London, 1993); M. Levey and G. Mandel, *Complete Paintings of Botticelli* (London, 1985); R. Lightbown, *Piero della Francesca* (New York, 1992); F. and S. Borsi, *Paolo Uccello* (in translation, London, 1994); R. Goffen, *Giovanni Bellini* (New Haven, 1989); V. Sgarbi, *Carpaccio* (in translation, New York, 1995); J. Martineau (ed.), *Andrea Mantegna* (London, 1992); M. Cardaro (ed.), *Mantegna's Camera degli Sposi* (Milan, 1993); C. Acidini Luchinat (ed.), *Gozzoli's Chapel of the Magi* (London,

1993); J. A. Becherer (ed.), *Pietro Perugino* (New York, 1997); C. Fischer, *Fra Bartolommeo* (Rotterdam, 1992); M. Clayton, *Raphael and his Studio* (London, 1999); C. Pedretti, *Raphael: his Life and Work* (Florence, 1989); A. E. Oppé, *Raphael* (London, 1970); L. D. and H. S. Ettlinger, *Raphael* (Oxford, 1987); J. Meyer zur Capellen, *Raphael in Florence* (London, 1996); *Michelangelo the Sculptor* (exhibition catalogue, Montreal, 1992); M. Hirst and J. Dunkerton, *The Young Michelangelo* (London, 1994); V. Manici, *Michelangelo the Painter* (New York, 1985); L. H. Collins and A. Ricketts, *Michelangelo* (London, 1991); Ludwig Goldscheider, *Michelangelo: Painter, Sculptor, Architect* (revised edition, Oxford, 1986); D. A. Brown, *Leonardo da Vinci: Origins of a Genius* (London, 1998), *Leonardo da Vinci: Engineer and Architect* (exhibition catalogue, Montreal, 1987), and *Leonardo and Venice* (Milan, 1992); A. E. Popham (ed.), *Notebooks of Leonardo* (revised edition, Oxford, 1994); Charles Hope, *Titian* (London, 1980); Hans Tietze, *Titian* (London, 1950); R. Goffen, *Titian's Women* (New Haven, 1994); S. S. Nigro, *Pontormo: Drawings* (New York, 1991), and *Pontormo: Paintings and Frescoes* (New York, 1993); David Ekserdjian, *Correggio* (London, 1997); Cecil Gould, *Parmigianino* (London, 1995); Ludwig Goldscheider, *Ghiberti* (London, 1949); Peter Streider, *Dürer* (London, 1982); and R. J. Schoeck, *Erasmus of Europe* (Edinburgh, 1990).

For drawings, so important for the study of Renaissance art, I have used especially the following collections: M. Jaffé, *The Devonshire Collection of Italian Drawings* (4 vols., London, 1994); F. Gibbons, *Italian Drawings in the Art Museum, Princeton* (2 vols., Princeton, 1977); J. Byam Shaw, *Italian Drawings in the Frits Lugt Collection* (3 vols., Paris, 1983), and *Drawings by Old Masters at Christ Church, Oxford* (2 vols., Oxford, 1976); J. Bean (ed.), *Fifteenth- and Sixteenth-Century Italian Drawings* (New York, 1982); *Renaissance Drawings from the Uffizi* (exhibition catalogue, New South Wales, 1995); N. Turner, *Florentine Drawings of the Sixteenth Century* (London, 1986); and J. Wilde, *Michelangelo and his Studio* (London, 1975). For the spread of the Renaissance in eastern and central Europe, I found illuminating Thomas DaCosta Kaufmann, *Court, Cloister and City: the Art and Culture of Central Europe, 1450–1800* (London, 1995).

Index